Doing the Right Thing at Work

Doing the Right Thing at Work

A CATHOLIC'S GUIDE TO FAITH, BUSINESS AND ETHICS

JAMES L. NOLAN

ST. ANTHONY MESSENGER PRESS

Cincinnati, Ohio

Excerpts from *Understanding Christian Spirituality* by Michael Downey, copyright ©1997 by Michael Downey, published by Paulist Press, Inc., New York/Mahwah, N.J. Used with permission of Paulist Press.
Excerpts from *Doors Into Prayer: An Invitation* by Emilie Griffin, Copyright ©2001 by Emilie Griffin. Used by permission of Paraclete Press. www.paracletepress.com.
Excerpts from *The Holy Longing: The Search for a Christian Spirituality* by Ronald Rolheiser, copyright ©1998 by Ronald Rolheiser. Used by permission of Doubleday, a Division of Random House, Inc.
English translation of the *Catechism of the Catholic Church Modifications from the Editio Typica,* copyright ©1997, United States Catholic Conference, Inc.—Libreria Editrice Vaticana. Used with permission.
Scripture passages have been taken from *New Revised Standard Version Bible*, copyright ©1989 by the Division of Christian Education of the National Council of the Churches of Christ in the U.S.A., and used by permission. All rights reserved.

Cover and book design by Mark Sullivan
Cover photo by Oleg Prikhodko/istockphoto

Library of Congress Cataloging-in-Publication Data

Nolan, James L., 1938-
Doing the right thing at work : a Catholic's guide to faith, business, and ethics / James L. Nolan.
p. cm.
Includes index.
ISBN 0-86716-676-2 (pbk. : alk. paper) 1. Christian ethics—Catholic authors. 2. Christian life—Catholic authors. 3. Work—Religious aspects—Christianity. I. Title.

BJ1249.N63 2006
241'.64—dc22

2006025791

ISBN-13 978-0-86716-676-7
ISBN-10 0-86716-676-2

Published by St. Anthony Messenger Press
28 W. Liberty St.
Cincinnati, OH 45202
www.AmericanCatholic.org

Printed in the United States of America
Printed on acid-free paper

06 07 08 09 10 5 4 3 2 1

Table of Contents

Dedication

For Karen, my wife and friend,
our wonderful children,
in-law children and grandchildren

ACKNOWLEDGMENTS

To the Woodstock Business Conference, its founders, board members, the many women and men who supported it with their wisdom, energy and financial resources, and, especially, to the coordinators, chaplains and participants in the Woodstock Business Conference chapters across North America, I say thank you. I am grateful for having been allowed to share in your stories and join in your movement.

I must acknowledge my gratitude to the Woodstock Theological Center at Georgetown University, to Rev. Gasper LoBiondo, S.J., its Director, and to Terry Armstrong, Ph.D., Director of its Arrupe Program in Business Ethics, for permission to use Woodstock Business Conference files, notes, minutes, manuals and articles so freely. Special thanks are due to Rev. Martin J. O'Malley, S.J., who organized and analyzed the transcripts of years of Business Conference meetings. He found in the record of those chapter meetings support for a model business leader, one whose leadership embodies the virtues of authenticity, loyalty, justice, faith, hope, love and prudence. For his work with the transcripts, editorial contributions, and superb insights, this book relies upon Fr. O'Malley's manuscript *The Corporate Christian: The Soul of a Leader* (Washington, D.C.: Woodstock Theological Center, 2004). Special thanks are also due to Rev. William J. Byron, S.J., whose sage counsel and impressive accomplishments across a breathtaking spectrum of jobs and roles have inspired so many. I thank as well my former colleague Michael J. Stebbins, Ph.D. His unique efforts in theology and ethics helped recognize and identify touchpoints embedded in the lives and work of the many talented and dedicated Woodstock Business Conference participants.

My deepest gratitude goes to Rev. James L. Connor, S.J., who directed and inspired the Woodstock Theological Center while I was privileged to serve as Executive Director of the Woodstock Business Conference. He labored long and hard to develop and articulate Woodstock's powerful process of theological reflection on experience. That process assists theologians and policymakers, academics and professionals in their work just as it aids us to grapple with the crucial issues that confront us each day. The Woodstock process holds great promise for all committed to doing the right thing at work and in the world.

INTRODUCTION

> Today, I was asked to increase someone's compensation. She had been talking to someone with a similar job at another company and realized that the person she was talking to made more than she was. So she came to me and asked what I thought about giving her a raise.
>
> How does my faith assist me in making a decision like that? What should I have been thinking of when I made my response to her? What should I have thought was fair? Is it simply what others pay or is there some criterion that I should have been able to discover from my Christian faith?
>
> I also have to consider beyond the needs of any particular employee the good of the firm even when it's a very good employee such as the woman who asked for the raise. And how do I balance out the firm's stability and good health with what may be a fair and just compensation to an employee?[1]

Doing the Right Thing at Work finds inspiration in the lives and stories of the men and women of the Woodstock Business Conference. Like the passage quoted above, it draws extensively upon their concrete experiences, their observations, insights, comments and questions. These Woodstock Business Conference conversations illustrate the lived experience of good people at work, the challenges they met, the lessons they learned and their desire to do the right thing. At the monthly Woodstock Business Conference meetings, they seriously consider their call, their vocation in the marketplace. They support and challenge one another along the way.

I know that challenge and that support. I was privileged to have participated in the meetings reported here and to have had a role in shaping the process that produced such fruitful and effective peer ministry. In the course of those meetings the truth is told, insights arise, patterns that encourage good authentic practices are identified and doing the right thing is encouraged.

This book is subtitled *A Catholic's Guide to Faith, Business and Ethics*. The desire to do the right thing is innate. It dominates whatever a person's worldview, governing philosophy or religious tradition might be. Certainly people can be just, kind, good whether they adhere to a particular religious faith or none at all. Because I have found such guidance, stimulus and nourishment in the Christian gospel and the Catholic faith community, in gratitude, I draw upon those rich resources for this effort. I write in the hope that all, including those of other dispositions, will follow along to see if some of what is said might resonate with their experience and understanding.

In a given situation our doing the right thing might be the result of good habits cultivated over a lifetime or might come about only after periods of trial and error, painful soul-searching and courageous risk-taking. Ultimately, doing the right thing results from a decision, a judgment that is itself informed by an understanding of the totality of a given situation. That understanding, in turn, depends upon our ability to grasp and explain the relevant facts and questions at hand. This is a lot of work to do; but sometimes, because of our training, experience and virtuous habits, the path from initial experience to decision and action can be almost instantaneous—it can happen in a flash. However long or short the process, it all begins with experience. And, so does this book.

As I hope the accounts in this book will illustrate, experience is the key to understanding, deciding and acting on our desire to do the right thing at work as well as in the rest of our lives. So, we begin in chapter one with a discussion about taking a stand on doing the right thing at work. We ask: How do we find our "moral compass"? We next look inside to see what is driving us as we try to figure out and do what is right. In chapter two we explore the fire that drives us. Chapter three takes up the question of the relevance, if any, of our religious faith to business practice. In chapter four we turn to the question of Christian spirituality in our work lives. Our focus shifts in chapter five from our individual situations to the world we live and work in, our workplace culture. Chapter six examines the reality and implications of our call to beneficially influence that culture.

A five-point program for doing the right thing results from our reflection and finding our moral compass. As we understand what drives us, how religious faith informs us and the implications in our workplace cultures, a program for wholeness and integrity emerges that includes:

- Self-awareness
- Expanding our horizons
- Engagement
- Community
- Prayer

Chapter seven gives an overview of this five-point program and considers the first point, self-awareness. Chapter eight explores the question of our horizons. What is it that we know and care about? What are the demands of social justice, our right relationships with others? Chapter nine turns to the necessity of engagement with the moral and ethical problems at work. The essential need for community and prayer are covered in chapters ten and eleven, respectively. The conclusion summarizes the main points of the book.

Since so much of this book draws upon the insights and fellowship of the Woodstock Business Conference groups, that organization, its formation, mission, process and administration are discussed at length in Appendix 1.

Each chapter ends with an exercise. These exercises can be used individually or as part of a study or reflection group. Because the key to understanding and deciding the right thing to do depends upon a comprehensive appreciation of our own experience, the exercises and insights they might promote can be as important as anything said in the text.

Pope John Paul II reminded us that we are called to sanctify the world by what we do at work and how we do it. It is my hope that this book and its exercises will help you to answer that call competently, faithfully and enthusiastically.

Chapter 1

Finding a Moral Compass

> He must have felt awful. Here was Jesus' right-hand man, the one groomed to lead his band of followers, the one who showed such determination, loyalty and strength; and he blew it.[1]

The participants gathered this afternoon to consider various opportunities for and challenges to doing the right thing in business. They came from positions of responsibility in business, the professions and government. Each month they gathered to encourage each other to "do the right thing" in their business lives. Following their regular practice, the group began by reading, reflecting silently upon and then discussing the Scripture passage that leads off each meeting. This time the Scripture focused on Saint Peter, always a favorite of the group, because he mirrors so well their very human aspirations, gifts and failings.

They began with a familiar scene, one reported in each of the four Gospels. There in the high priest's courtyard, just as Jesus predicted it would happen, Peter denied knowing Jesus three times. Then, the rooster crowed after the third denial. Peter failed to stand up for Jesus despite his earlier promises of undying fidelity.

A vice president of an international electronic equipment firm opened the conversation, saying, "This passage tells me that in our business lives we should stand up for what we believe. It doesn't have to be a popular sentiment." Later, he would recount a time when doing the right thing meant that he had to risk his position in his company by standing up for what he believed in a particularly troubling situation.

Another participant spoke up:

> The thing I take from this story is that Peter put himself at risk. He was the only disciple there in the courtyard. The others had fled. He was probably scared half to death, knowing it was not going well for his friend Jesus who was inside right then on trial for his life. Peter was in a very difficult place. He must have felt terrible when he denied even knowing Jesus. Peter was just a man. He was trying to get through the night. And, he does not come out looking very good.

Several others agreed that Peter was in a no-win situation. It was futile. He was in no position to change things. "What could he do there, anyway?" "On the other hand," one added, "that kind of rationalization is only too familiar to all of us. It is human to try to rationalize in order to get out of becoming involved in a mess."

The Scripture discussion carried over into the comments on the topic for the day, which was "What happens to a company's benevolent practices when it faces hard times?" As the conversation progressed, a very successful woman, whose company was the leader in its field, offered this telling insight: "It seems that Peter's story applies to each of us. We have similar fears, similar confusions. We are sometimes at a loss to know the right thing to do, particularly when we hit difficult times. Today, the question is how do we either find or refind our moral compass when we need to act? There has to be a bridge somewhere."

The vice president who said he knew he had to stand up for what he believed told of his meeting with his CEO and the senior leadership of his company. He laid out the pros and cons for the full public disclosure and the remedial action he believed the situation required. His company had to properly address a highly publicized, problematic corporate action that had taken place many decades before. He went into the meeting knowing of entrenched opposition to his proposal and believing that his job was on the line. He admitted that he was scared. As it turned out, his advice carried the day and a grateful CEO praised him. Not all cases turn out so favorably. This is particularly true where the survival of a firm is at risk. Nevertheless, this executive, like Saint Peter after Pentecost, ultimately found the resources to do the right thing.

The familiar account of Peter's denial of Jesus in Luke's Gospel concludes: "The Lord turned and looked at Peter. Then Peter remembered the word of the Lord, how he had said to him, 'Before the cock crows today, you will deny me three times.' And he went out and wept bitterly" (Luke 22:61–62).

Peter wept bitterly because he realized that he came up short. He failed to stand up for Jesus. He let his good friend down and felt crushing shame. If this incident had marked the end of Peter's work as a follower of Christ and leader of Christ's community, he would have been an abject failure. He knew it. However, as one after another of the Woodstock participants added, Peter's story does not stop there. Peter returns to the community of Jesus' followers. They huddle in the Upper Room, quaking with fear. Later, huffing and puffing, Peter chases John back to the tomb to follow up on Mary Magdalene's report that the body was missing and that she had seen the risen Lord. Peter returned to the community as its acknowledged leader. He, too, experienced Jesus after the Resurrection. The Lord told him three times to feed his lambs and his sheep. Peter was there at the Lord's final leave-taking. And, returning again to the Upper Room, just as the Lord had promised would happen, he and the others received the Holy Spirit. The Pentecost event blasted him out of his fearful hiding and into the temple square to proclaim the gospel.

Jesus did not give up on Peter. Rather, he kept after him, asking Peter to affirm his love and commitment as he charged him to care for his flock. Peter found his moral compass and went to work with newfound courage and vitality.

Toward the end of the meeting, a senior member of the group said he found an answer to the question of doing the right thing, finding one's moral compass, in the story of Peter:

> What caused Peter to turn around? As I see it, when Jesus looked at Peter standing there in the courtyard, their eyes locked and their personal relationship came alive. Peter was a man who Jesus loved and respected very deeply. When they looked at each other, Peter saw someone he really loved. He must have recalled their times together. He must have remembered the community in which they shared their lives and values together. It all came alive in that look.

Indeed, that look must have triggered memories for Peter, of how Jesus taught him and the others, how he trusted Peter and opened himself to Peter. Peter realized that what he had done was not up to snuff. He was surely scared, and very confused about what was happening. Standing in that courtyard he may well have thought, "What good will it do now by admitting to being Jesus' friend and follower?" But when their eyes locked, that was the connection to bring him back to his life's solid-rock foundation as the Lord's chief disciple. Peter remembered, wept, repented, regained his moral compass and returned to lead his community. He continued his close personal engagement with the Risen Christ. When push came to shove, the values of the Lord, his community and the people he loved guided Peter's actions.

As we will explore in the pages that follow, Peter's story, his whole story, does apply to us. We do have similar fears, similar confusions. We are sometimes at a loss to know the right thing to do when we need to act. We, too, can find or recover our moral compass the same way Peter did by remembering, weeping and repenting when it's called for, and then going back to work. We can do the right thing at work because we are sustained by the Lord and by our communities of love. Our communities of love can include our families, our friends, the people we work with and serve, and our faith community. For Catholics, that faith community includes two thousand years of fellow followers of Christ. The foundation for this sustaining, nurturing, instructing and challenging love is found in the love and confidence Christ has in each of us and in the hope and the gratitude that erupts in us from our realization and acceptance of Christ's love. "Hope does not disappoint us, because God's love has been poured into our hearts through the Holy Spirit that has been given to us" (Romans 5:5).

The themes that echoed that day are fairly representative of the concerns of serious-minded businessmen and businesswomen trying to do the right thing:

- standing up for what you believe at work when times are tough,
- being scared and confused on occasion,
- confronting seemingly futile situations,
- needing persistence after falling short, and
- regaining one's moral compass.

These are typical of Woodstock Business Conference conversations across the country. It is my hope that these themes, or some of them, are familiar to you as well.

Peter got back on course after he was jolted into remembering his love and respect for his friend Jesus and his deep desire to serve him. He did not quit but remained faithful to his particular call to serve the community of disciples. Indeed,

Peter's persistence was so strong that nothing could stop him. The Acts of the Apostles (4:5–21) reports that when he was on trial before the Sanhedrin in Jerusalem, Peter told the leaders of the Jewish community that he simply could not stop speaking out about what he had seen and heard despite their order to stop teaching about Jesus.

The question about finding our moral compass is a serious one. When we are tugged in so many different directions at work, we need a moral compass to guide us in making the right decision and moving forward. We want to do the right thing for our company, our neighbors and ourselves. One lesson from this conversation is that we, too, can get back on course:

- by remembering,
- being persistent, and
- acting in line with our deepest desires to serve God.

Test this lesson against your own experience and see if it rings true.

Exercise

Our stories count. In this exercise see how your experience might match the story of Saint Peter's ordeal in the courtyard with which we began.

1. Quiet yourself. Be aware that you are in God's presence.

2. Ask for the grace to experience God's loving companionship and to respond in gratitude.

3. Recall a time at work when you were put in a position where you needed to take a stand and do the right thing. Remember the details of the situation—when, where, who, how and why. As you remember the events, take note of the feelings that went along with the raw data. Jot down notes, if that helps to fix the circumstances in your mind.

4. Next, read one of the accounts of Saint Peter in the high priest's courtyard (Matthew 26:69–75; Mark 14:66–72; Luke 22:56–63; or John 18:15–18, 25–27). With your mind's eye put yourself into the scene. Try to sense the noise, the darkness, the chill and the smell of the fire. Listen as the various characters confront Peter. Hear his answers. Try to be aware of what was going on inside him at the time.

5. Talk to God about your situation and Saint Peter's. Are they similar, different? How do they end? How would you want them to end? What, if anything, do you want to do next? Tell God what you want.

6. Close by thanking God for any insights gained, truths learned. Pray the Our Father.

CHAPTER 2
THE FIRE THAT DRIVES US

We know deep inside that we must rely upon our moral compass when we need to act. We have seen that we need to remember, take stock and get back to work in line with our deepest desires. We have to get to work in order to get the job done, of course. But there is something even more basic than the particular task at hand. What we do when confronted with a challenging difficulty or uncertainty at work serves to determine who we are. In any given circumstance, our action will be the product of the fire that drives us and the habits and disciplines we have developed over time to channel and direct our desire for completeness and wholeness.

The Fire Within

How do we know this is so? One way is to check the evidence we have within us. At one time or another, we all have experienced a dynamic power inside us that moves us to seek what is true. While we do not do it all the time, we ask pertinent questions—who, what, when, where and how—when a problem arises. We somehow need to get the facts right. That drive to get the story straight seems to be built right into us. We can also sense an internal dynamic that pushes us to choose what is valuable and worthwhile. We want to know the truth and to do what is right. One does not have to be a believer to be asking questions and making judgments. We are doing it all the time. It is a part of being alive.

Just what is the source of this dynamic in us? The life energy that drives us shows up in our desire to do the right thing. But the same driving life force can also push us astray, away from God toward other gods we would worship and serve. The false gods beckoning us include fame, power and fortune. Ultimately, what we do with this life force is key to our integration or disintegration as persons.

An expert on contemporary Christian life, Ronald Rolheiser, O.M.I., holds that this internal desire is so important that the wholeness of our lives is determined by what we do with it. The life habits and disciplines we fashion over time to channel and direct this desire shape us.[1] In *The Holy Longing*, his inspiring book on the spiritual life, Rolheiser says:

> Desire makes us act and when we act what we do will either lead to a greater integration or disintegration within our personalities, minds, and bodies—and to the strengthening or deterioration of our relationship to God, others, and to the cosmic world. The habits and disciplines we use to shape our desire form the basis for spirituality, regardless of whether these have an explicit religious dimension to them or whether they are consciously expressed at all.[2]

Christians recognize that this drive—this interior desire to determine what is good and what is not, what is fair and not, what is right and what is wrong, what truly respects the dignity of human beings and what diminishes that dignity—is God working in our ordinary, everyday lives. People of faith have long recognized that God's law and the desire to live it is written on our hearts. It is an integral part of us. We need only turn to the summary chapters of Deuteronomy to see how Moses laid this out for his people as they were about to enter the Promised Land.

> Surely, this commandment that I am commanding you today is not too hard for you, nor is it too far away. It is not in heaven, that you should say, "Who will go up to heaven for us, and get it for us so that we may hear it and observe it?" Neither is it beyond the sea, that you should say, "Who

> will cross to the other side of the sea for us, and get it for us so that we may hear it and observe it?" No, the word is very near to you; it is in your mouth and in your heart for you to observe. (Deuteronomy 30:11–14)

With the image of the law and love of God etched in our hearts, we can say that we are God-seeking creatures, driven to union with God. This ancient Biblical image is another way of saying that we are hardwired to quest for God, on and off the job. Interestingly, a geneticist has even suggested that our capacity for spirituality is, in fact, a part of our genetic makeup. Geneticist Dean H. Hamer, author of *The God Gene: How Faith Is Hardwired into Our Genes*,[3] was quoted saying, "We think that all human beings have an innate capacity for spirituality and that that desire to reach out beyond oneself, which is at the heart of spirituality, is a part of the human makeup."[4]

Whether we have an identifiable gene for it or not, we can recognize that this desire to reach beyond ourselves mobilizes and propels us. We must also acknowledge that we are free to choose and can aim elsewhere. We can reject God's drive in us. We can run from him or deaden ourselves to this loving and dynamic attraction to him. Father Rolheiser has many ways to describe this drive. He calls it variously a push, dynamism, the eros and the fire inside us. He cites John of the Cross, the great Spanish mystic, who begins his famous treatment of the soul's journey with the words, "One dark night, fired by love's urgent longings...." For John of the Cross and Father Rolheiser, it is love's urgent longings, the eros, the desires that are the starting point of the complete and integrated life.

Another contemporary theologian and scholar of Christian spirituality, Michael Downey, says something quite similar. He calls the dynamic drive the universal quest for integration and completion through self-transcending knowledge, freedom and love. He claims that:

> Christian spirituality is most profitably understood viewed in the context of the more basic and fundamental human quest for integration of mind, body and soul.…Christian life in the Spirit is a particular, indeed unique, expression of the universal human desire for integration and completion through self-transcending knowledge, freedom and love.[5]

From all sides we see that our desire for completeness, for wholeness, the drive to integrate all of who we are including, particularly, who and what we are at work, is the engine that drives us to fulfill our destiny.

Often it is in our guts that we get a good sense of what these experts are talking about. It happens at work when we seek to excel, when we thrill at doing our job, when we fall short and we know it, and even when we are being pulled in different directions. Work can be the occasion for some very strong feelings such as elation, excitement, satisfaction as well as dread, foreboding and regret. These feelings point to the fire within us and can, depending upon the habits and disciplines we have followed, help signal whether or not we are on the right path to integration and completion, whether we are on course to doing the right thing.

Channeling the Fire at Work

The fire within that drives us, and we hope moves us to greater completeness and integration, is not merely some abstract concept. We do not do it alone. We can only achieve greater integration through living, working, struggling and confronting situations, problems and dilemmas in life. As we do so, we grow and work out who we are. When we grab for our moral compass and pursue our desire to do the right thing at work, we are moving toward greater integration and authenticity. However, the fact that we are fallible humans means that we also carry blinders. We make choices that move us away from integration toward disintegration and decline. We can be egotistic, selfish, inattentive, lazy, forgetful and fearful. We can be blind to God's counsel and deaf to the Word written on our hearts. In short, we can sin.

And, as Father Rolheiser notes, "How we channel our eros [desire]...the disciplines and habits we choose to live by, will either lead to a greater integration or disintegration."[6] For most of us, our workplaces are the arenas where this channeling takes place. Our work is much more than a job category or pay grade. It is where our choices enforce the disciplines and habits that ultimately determine who we are. This is where we know, choose and do what is best. But we are not simply involved in the process of our working out who we are in our workplaces. What we do at work can promote God's agenda. *Work is a place where we can truly team up with God.* God is already there. His Holy Spirit labors in us, and moves us to exert our gifts and powers for the greater good.

This working out of who we are is not done in a vacuum. We are social creatures. Our work life is seldom a solitary pursuit. We are all linked with God's other creatures as we work in the world. All business and commerce boils down to a cooperative exchange in one form or another. On the job we readily see the need for cooperation and coordination. At work we know that "we are all in this together." We have to find ways of workplace engagement that honor our shared birthright and mission.

The question of business ethics is a very practical form of working out who we are in the company of our fellow creatures. The Woodstock Theological Center in its recent projects exploring the ethics of lobbying asserts that ethics is really a method of learning and doing in the everyday, concrete reality of our lives. This important process of working out ethics and morals merits special concern because it regards very fundamental questions about:

- the type of persons we should become,
- the kinds of communities we should create,
- what we should do and avoid doing,
- the rights and responsibilities of human beings,
- the range of goods—social, economic, cultural, personal, spiritual—that are necessary for human well being, and
- the gradations of good and evil (why some goods are more important and some evils more dangerous than others).[7]

Business ethics is not a laundry list of isolated rules, separate and apart from the actors involved. But rather, ethics is a measure of our living and doing in terms of our relationships and responsibilities. Ethics, often discussed in sterile and impersonal terms, is at the very heart of who we are as persons and how we relate to each other and the rest of God's creation.

The same life force that is key to our personal spirituality, our integration or disintegration as individuals, our drive to be in relationship with God, is central to our ethics, the working out of who we are in the company of our fellow creatures. This life force, the fire within, powers us in determining who we are as individuals and how we relate to God and our fellow creatures. Our challenge is how we manage and direct the process. What are the disciplines and habits that promote our staying on the right path, that promote our integration and protect us against disintegration?

Naming the Disciplines and Habits

As a step to naming the disciplines and habits that work to support a Catholic businessperson, the directors of the Woodstock Business Conference held a series of meetings to explore the ethical dynamism at work in the lives of serious, competent businesspeople. The first meeting focused on understanding the dynamics at work when good business decisions are made. The goal was to identify the structures and operations that promote decisions and actions done well. What is happening when someone operates at his best? Each member of the Woodstock Business Conference board came with a concrete example, one occasion where he or she concluded that a good decision was made. One member, a banker, gave an account of a challenging situation where he thought he got it right. In this instance, he properly analyzed a situation, assigned responsibility appropriately, saved jobs and protected his bank from damaging losses.

> I've been a banker for thirty-one years. I think the best work I did, or that I was a part of, was during the last real estate meltdown. The chairman of the bank asked me if I would try to solve a problem we had at the bank with bad real estate loans. We had a little over $2 billion in real estate loans. With the market collapsing, an awful lot of that was either troublesome loans or about to become troublesome loans. We had a serious meeting with the board regarding the size of the problem. The first thing the board wanted to do was fire all the people who caused the problem. We are talking about 150 men and women in this real estate business. The board felt that somehow these people did something inappropriate in originating the loans.
>
> The first thing I had to do was to convince the board that the human beings who made the loans were not responsible for the problem. The problem was: (1) the market collapsed and (2) the board not only allowed for this huge concentration to occur, but when the market was good, it encouraged the making of the loans because

> they looked very profitable. So, the first thing was to tell the board members that it was their fault and that the 150 people should not be summarily fired.
>
> But, even if we didn't want to blame the people who originated the loans, could those same people solve the problem? Solving the problem required very difficult negotiations to work out payments with the borrowers; and once you went through that process, then came the foreclosure process to liquidate the real estate. These folks did not have that experience. The choice was to fire all our real estate people and hire "workout specialists" for the workout process, then fire those people, and hire "foreclosure specialists" for the liquidation part. Or, we could retrain our real estate people to handle the new assignment. We chose the latter.
>
> Over about a three-year period, we were able to liquidate about $1.2 billion worth of real estate loans with the same people going through various cycles of having originated, then working out and then liquidating.
>
> I was particularly pleased with that because I thought that we were able to identify who was responsible for the problem and not to punish the innocent. We not only preserved their jobs for a period of time, but also put them in a position to expand their own capability and experience. The whole process ended up being a very successful activity.[8]

Consider what is going on as this story unfolds. One can feel the verve and drive that energized the banker. He was alive. He was on top of his game. His adrenaline was pumping. He might have had more than a little apprehension as he approached the board members with his assessment that they were the ones who bore responsibility for the problem. The chairman called for the best of his skills and talents, and he delivered. Where did he get his determination to assess the causes of the situation properly, to manage it, protect people's jobs and insure the viability of his bank? Where did the banker's concern for his people come from? How did he have the freedom to generate options where others equally concerned for the welfare of the bank might simply have frozen? When asked about this, the banker acknowledged that it was, indeed, a frightening situation, one where there was a real concern for possible failure. The viability of the bank, as well as his own job, were at stake.

He cited his years of experience and successful management of banking enterprises. He recognized the scope of the challenge and knew what he was doing. He knew he had to assess the question of responsibility properly and to articulate his conclusion in a convincing fashion. It was not easy to put responsibility right back in the board's lap. It was, however, the right thing to do. After that, he said with characteristic modesty, "The rest was process."

The work habits and disciplines formed over the years served him well as he demonstrated hard work, careful analysis, forthright communication and openness to unconventional options. His was leadership at its best. Habits and disciplines gave him the freedom to name the truth, to see what had to be done and the courage to act.

When pushed as to how he was able to come to the right decision and carry it out, he also acknowledged that his Catholic faith promoted certain virtues and habits in his life. It helped him to recognize and take account of others and to be concerned about their development. He said that his faith gave him the freedom to name the truth, to see what had to be done and the courage to act.

Over the years this banker had so channeled the fire within him, had so honed the habits and disciplines upon which he had to rely, that he was able to respond to a very challenging situation competently, vigorously and courageously.

Exercise

The purpose of this exercise is to get in touch with the fire burning within you in the context of a time at work when you made and carried out a good business decision.

1. Begin by thanking God for life, for providing you with opportunities to experience his grace within your heart.

2. Read Moses' final charge to the Israelites in Deuteronomy 30:11–14 quoted in this chapter. Couple that with the words of Saint Paul from Romans 5:5: "Hope does not disappoint us, because God's love has been poured into our hearts through the Holy Spirit that has been given to us."

3. Recall a time at work when you confronted a difficulty or uncertainty and you know that you did the right thing. Recall what questions you asked, what information you needed and what data you gathered. Think about your analysis of the problems and of the judgments you made. Recall the action(s) you took.

4. Take note of what was going on inside as you went through the whole process. Did you feel yourself really in tune with what was right and worthwhile?

5. Thank God for the grace of that occasion. Say the Glory Be to the Father.

CHAPTER 3

THE RELEVANCE OF RELIGIOUS FAITH TO BUSINESS PRACTICE

The disciplines and habits we develop over a lifetime can channel our internal drive so that we can grow toward greater integration and wholeness. Our work lives often set the stage where this development takes place. The banker in the last chapter credited his religious faith with promoting those habits of thought and action that enabled him to successfully address a very difficult challenge to his bank.

The claim that underlies this book is captured in the motto of the Woodstock Business Conference, "Affirming the Relevance of Religious Faith to Business Practice." This is a rather bold claim to make at any time and particularly so at the present. How did this claim come about? What is this Woodstock process that enables so many to see its motto fulfilled in their work lives? What can be gleaned from the experience of Woodstock participants that is of general applicability and usefulness to Catholic men and women in the marketplace today—how to know and do the right thing when we need to act?

How Did the Claim Come About?

Business ethics is about doing the right thing in the context of the business transaction, enterprise or firm. It means making decisions and taking actions with the interests of all stakeholders in mind. As they address the needs of their companies, people in business, entrepreneurs and professionals are constantly making moral decisions that affect their companies, coworkers and the wider community. In doing so, they shape their own lives as well. In deciding the right thing to do, business people easily affirm that ethical and moral values provide them with guides for decision-making. Ethical and moral values also gird the structures and systems that support the conduct of all trade and commerce, though less visibly so. One question, however, keeps recurring: Where are these values to be found? As the participant in the conversation about Saint Peter's denial asked, "How does one locate her moral compass?" When questioned about a particular business decision or action, thoughtful men and women are often unable to articulate fully the moral and ethical values grounding the "decision." Theirs are often "gut decisions," judgments that come from resources deep within based upon a lifetime of habits.

While everyone may want to do the right thing and all can support the idea of ethical and moral values being worthwhile, our pluralistic, secular culture discounts and frequently denies the relevance of religious faith to business practice. The prevailing assumption in business, as in most contemporary activities in America, is that there must be a wall of separation. It is assumed that this wall is required because we do not all share the same faith-based worldview. Our society demands respect for the personal and deeply held beliefs of others. Failure to tolerate others' views smacks of bigotry and puts people at a commercial disadvantage. No one wants to be branded as oppressive, outmoded or quirky.

People often draw sharp lines between spirituality and religion. Spirituality is seen as good, as that which really matters. Religion and adherence to the beliefs of a religious tradition are suspect. But for people of faith, religion holds meaning. It is not perceived as an oppressor of personal freedom. One's faith can be a trusted path by which to approach one's ultimate goal in life, eternal life with the loving God. As such, our religious faith and traditions are highly relevant to what we do at work, as in all aspects of life. Indeed, the church draws our attention to two important aspects of this reality:

- Work is where we exercise and fulfill our God-given gifts and talents.
- Work is where we team up with God for the good of others and his creation.

The first relates to our growth and maturity as persons. Work is terribly important not just for the wages we earn, but because, as we have seen, it is the arena where we exercise and fulfill the God-given gifts and talents that are our potential.[1] As we grow and better realize our gifts we become more and more authentically human, more and more integrated, more and more what God has created us to be. When our work "...honors the Creator's gifts and talents received from him. It can also be redemptive."[2] Again, it is in the everyday challenges at our workplaces that we know, choose and do what is best. These are the occasions and opportunities for us to develop the habits and disciplines needed to grow in integration of mind, body and spirit.

Second, our personal spiritual maturity, while good in itself, is not the end of the story. We are God's creations who are called to be God's coworkers in God's project. We are invited to use our intelligence, our energy, our savvy and all that we care about to that end. When we do so, when we understand and choose the positive and recognize and work to diminish the negative, when we work and make life better in any way—we are not doing it alone. We are in league with God, being led by the Holy Spirit who is working within and through us. God is working in us and moving us to work for the greater good.

The church at the Second Vatican Council said it this way in *Lumen gentium* reflecting on the role and calling of men and women at work:

> But by reason of their special vocation it belongs to the laity to seek the kingdom of God by engaging in temporal affairs and directing them according to God's will. They live in the world, that is, they are engaged in each and every work and business of the earth and in the ordinary circumstances of social and family life which, as it were constitute their very existence. There they are called by God that, being led by the spirit of the Gospel, they may contribute to the sanctification of the world, as from within like leaven, by fulfilling their own particular duties....It pertains to them in a special way so to illuminate and order all temporal things with which they are so closely associated that these may be affected and grow according to Christ and may be the glory of the Creator and Redeemer.[3]

The Judeo-Christian tradition has long understood our work in the world as a calling or vocation. This tradition highlights the fact that businesspersons, managers, entrepreneurs or professionals are stewards, entrusted with God's creation. Called to employ one's God-given talents and skills, he or she manages the assets at his or her disposal for the creation and distribution of wealth, employment, products and services. They need to be able to perform with skill and competence.

The claim that our faith is relevant to business came about from a realization of who we are, what we are called to be and how we go about growing in integration and spiritual maturity. It is in business, at our offices and workplaces where most of us realize our gifts and grow to maturity. It is in the particularity of our work lives that many of us are called to mission, to work with God, to "illuminate and order things" so that who and what we encounter will grow according to Christ. These messages tell us that our job is to contribute to the sanctification of the world and to manifest Christ to others by the witness of our lives everywhere and particularly at work. It is a very challenging task if we are to answer this call to mission, and to do it well.

The fact is that many Catholics do not easily see what they do at work as a vocation. Vocation has long been thought to refer exclusively to the call to Holy Orders and the religious life. For many of us, our work is just a job or maybe a career but in no way a holy call. What the church is telling us, however, is that whatever we do we are called by God and have a job to contribute to the sanctification of the world, whatever our particular occupation. For this reason who we are and what we do is, or should be, a vocation and our response to God's call. To be called by God in our work means that more than material rewards (wages, compensation) or psychic rewards (personal growth and satisfaction) are at stake. It also encompasses the social and spiritual aspirations of our Christian lives.

One of the Woodstock participants, the business owner, talked about what it meant for him to see his work as a vocation.

> I think about how my decisions will affect the corporation, about the staff who rely on us for their livelihood and about the complexity of what used to be simple problems.... For me ethics in business is making difficult decisions—and we are all faced with them—and doing the right thing. Sometimes there is not a lot of guidance about what is right. But if I listen to others and check my internal compass, I usually figure it out.[4]

The topic for the meeting that day was "What values do you call upon to guide you in a chaotic, fluid, changing set of circumstances?" Before recalling a recent situation to illustrate his point, this participant noted that he was known in and outside his firm as a Catholic businessperson. Others, he said, expected that his Christian values would inform the decisions he made in his business, and he expected it of himself. He brought up a dilemma he had recently faced. He instituted a number of "hard-and-fast rules" on hiring. They were to be strictly enforced to protect against unwarranted employment and discrimination claims. One rule was that job offers had to be accepted at the "salary we pay" or the offer was withdrawn. Period. No exceptions. His dilemma that day was such that he felt he had to make an exception to his firm rule.

> In our New York office a young woman was interviewed and offered a job at a salary that she did not accept. She was under the misunderstanding that she could go home and think over the offer. But you see we had this rule that we do not negotiate, period. This was obviously not made clear to her, because she came back to the office and accepted the salary that was offered. But, the personnel employee in charge of hiring told the woman the job she had applied for had been given to somebody else. This was not true. It was a lie that protected the personnel employee from explaining the "hard-and-fast rule" that our company doesn't accept negotiating of salaries. When I learned about this, I found out that we have a weakness in our management in New York. I realized that we were wrong. We didn't explain our rules to the prospective employee, and worst of all, we lied. So I decided to make it clear to hire the woman anyway because we have to tell the truth. It is a Christian value to be concerned with people and to be truthful. I hope my managers can learn through my actions that some other values exist and not just the letter of one of our hard-and-fast rules. If you talk about Christian values, it is something that is connected with people almost every time.[5]

On another occasion this same business owner had more to say about the importance of connecting people with business ethics:

> Finally, ethics in business is recognizing the special relationship you have with your employees. I am dependent on them to make me successful. They are dependent on me for their financial well-being. The decisions I make will affect their future. It is my job to find the balance of maintaining my standards and expectations for performance, but respecting the individual employees and their personal situations. Sometimes it is hard to balance.[6]

The man quoted here recognized that his was a calling and responded to that call as a good steward. He was well aware of his responsibilities and the challenges that came with them. He showed his true colors in his business and personal life. A remarkable man, he frequently said that for him business was fun and exciting. He relished competition and the challenges. He was also an extremely generous person, a model husband and father. Those who know him appreciate the importance and relevance of his religious faith and understand that he expects to be judged by the standards his faith demands. He serves as a model of the integration we all seek. He freely admits his good fortune as he helps others by sharing widely and empowering many. We are not all going to be so fortunate. Yet, we can all recognize our calling, our vocation to illuminate and order the practices and institutions with which we are closely associated so that they that they may be affected and grow according to Christ.

Exercise

1. After setting aside time for quiet and grateful acknowledgment of God's presence in your life, begin by reading slowly the Scripture passage below (Matthew 6:24–29, 33–34) where Jesus talks about the difficulty of serving two masters and highlights what our real concerns should be.

> No one can serve two masters; for a slave will either hate the one and love the other, or be devoted to the one and despise the other. You cannot serve God and wealth.
>
> Therefore, I tell you, do not worry about your life, what you will eat or what you will drink, or about your body, what you will wear. Is not life more than food and the body more than clothing? Look at the birds of the air; they neither sow nor reap nor gather into barns, and yet your heavenly Father feeds them. Are you not of more value than they? And can any of you by worrying add a single hour to your span of life? And why do you worry about clothing? Consider the lilies of the field, how they grow; they neither toil nor spin, yet I tell you, Solomon in all his glory was not clothed like one of these....But strive first for the kingdom of God and his righteousness, and all these things will be given to you as well.
>
> So do not worry about tomorrow, for tomorrow will bring worries of its own. Today's trouble is enough for today.

2. Next, consider these questions. Take them up one at a time.
   - Do you bring Christian values to your work?
   - Are you expected to do so by those who know you?
   - Do you expect yourself to?
   - Is it realistic to expect us to be living our "vocation" in our work, firm or business?
   - Do economics, productivity, competitiveness and the need for efficiency permit us to consider Christian values at work?
   - Where in your work can you illuminate and order the things with which you are closely associated so that they may be affected and grow according to Christ?

3. Take a moment to reflect on what, if anything, struck you as you were considering these questions. Talk to God about it and ask what you are to do next.

4. Then, thank God for his call to you. Pray this prayer from Saint Teresa of Avila:

> *Let nothing disturb you,*
> *Nothing frighten you,*
> *All things are passing.*
> *God never changes.*
> *Patient endurance attains all things.*
> *Whoever possesses God lacks nothing–*
> *God alone is sufficient.*
> *Amen.*

CHAPTER 4

A CHRISTIAN SPIRITUALITY OF WORK

The fire that burns within us not only drives us to find and clutch our moral compass but also spurs us to achieve. We reach for the stars to realize our God-given potential. Striving to be the best we can be and pursuing excellence in our lives can be a grand adventure. It can be an authentic response to God's call, and that can be seen as Christian spirituality at work. Here we turn to explore the question of Christian spirituality in our work lives. We try to understand what the idea of spirituality addresses in our lives, what marks Christian spirituality and what the demands might be if we are to embrace Christian spirituality at work. Once again, answers emerge as Woodstock businesspeople discuss important issues in light of their experiences in the workplace.

One afternoon a Woodstock group met to discuss what made an excellent company. A meaty article by James C. Collins and Jerry I. Porras, "Building Your Company's Vision" (*Harvard Business Review*, September/October, 1996), summarized the main points in their seminal book, *Built to Last: Successful Habits of Visionary Companies,*[1] and set the stage for the conversation that followed.

The authors compared outstanding companies with successful companies in the same field and determined that those acknowledged to be excellent all had core values and purpose that remained fixed while their business strategies and practices adapted to a changing world. For example, they compared Bristol-Meyers and Johnson & Johnson. The authors concluded that Johnson & Johnson was an outstanding company, better over the long run in comparison with Bristol-Meyers, because it maintained a clear set of values and held to a purpose, that of promoting health. It was not just something they said in order to make money; it was the heart of their business.

Authors Collins and Porras concluded that great companies understand the difference between what should never change and what should be open for change. They argued that it was vision that provided the necessary guidance about what was at the center and had to be preserved and what to aim for in the future. The article describes vision as consisting of two major components:

1. Core values. This defines the enduring character of an organization—a consistent identity, in which certain values are the essential and enduring tenets of an organization, and purpose is the organization's reason for being.
2. Envisioned future. This is the famous call for a vision of "Big, Hairy, Audacious Goals." Big, hairy audacious goals (BHAG's) have to be bold, clear and compelling. They must be vividly described.

The discussion stimulated by this article began with a consideration of a passage from Scripture about the Great Commandment.

> "Teacher, which commandment in the law is the greatest?" He said to him: "'You shall love the Lord, your God with all your heart, and with your whole soul, and with all your mind.' This is the greatest and first commandment. The second is like it: 'You shall love your neighbor as yourself.' On these two commandments hang all the law and the prophets." (Matthew 22:36–40)

Having read the article and meditated on the Gospel passage, the first speaker remarked:

> This reminds me of two other passages. The first is "Seek ye first the kingdom, and all these other things will be

> given to you." It also reminds me of Joseph in the Book of Genesis. He always knew who he was and what his values were; he suffered reversals of fortune, but ultimately he prospered.
>
> I think it is true that in our lives there is a plan somehow working itself out, a wind behind our backs carrying us through. I often used to compartmentalize my faith—partly because it did not seem to help much when I prayed about my business or my relationships anyway! But doing it on my own didn't work either. I realize now I cannot just put my spiritual life on one side and the rest of my life on the other side. Somehow, I have to come back before the altar with everything and realize there is a mystery working itself out in my life.[2]

The next speaker observed:

> When I read the visionary companies article, it seemed like there was a prior question: Do I have core values and an envisioned future? Rather than looking at the company first, we have to be fully aware of who we are. We are important actors, bringing something to the company, helping it live out its vision.

A Quest—Spirituality at Work

These comments, prompted by an article on corporate excellence, meditation on the Great Commandment and reflections on personal experience form the heart of the quest for a Christian spirituality of work: We seek the integration of the whole of our lives.

This quest toward the ultimate is rooted in God disclosed in Jesus Christ.

The Holy Spirit, active and present in our hearts and the community of discipleship called the church, powers it.

God is drawing us into this journey in each and every part of our lives, including that part that takes up the majority of our time as adults; our work.

The quest drives us to action.

Based upon our experience and that of others at work, we can affirm that we are God-seekers who, with God's grace, have a chance to grow and choose wisely and rightly in the decisions we make, the actions we take and the people we become. Our work becomes a place for our spiritual growth. At work we can find spiritual growth as we attend to our moral compass. What we can find is a spirituality of work. According to Michael Downey, the two hallmarks of any spirituality are:

1. A conscious striving to integrate the whole of one's life through self-transcendence in the face of fragmentation and depersonalization in our world.
2. An awareness of "levels of reality not immediately apparent," the reality that is more than meets the eye.[3]

This somewhat vague and fuzzy description of spirituality is mandated by what Downey terms today's "spirituality sprawl": the flood of books, lectures, workshops, Web sites, practices, interests, products and beliefs all under the heading of "spirituality." All are one response or another to our craving for integration and to experience the sacred. One example, the July 9, 2001, issue of *Fortune* magazine ran an unusual cover story, "God and Business: The Surprising Quest for Spiritual Renewal in the American Workplace." *Fortune*'s managing editor justified this unusual topic for his magazine by quoting the reporter Marc Gunther as saying, "I was amazed at the number of business people, especially baby-boomers, looking for a higher purpose in their lives, willing to talk about their faith publicly, and trying to integrate it into their work."[4] The editor continued, "Marc has discovered something real that's affecting a surprising number of our readers, and he has presented it as what it is—a large, unorganized, deeply felt, and deeply personal movement."[5] The Woodstock participants that afternoon gave voice to their interest in spirituality, finding higher purpose and integrating their faith and work. That interest only grows. A recent Google search for the words "spirituality and work" produced over 4.6 million links!

Spiritual, But Not Religious

For many, the search for the integration beyond one's self can easily be seen as a spiritual journey but not a religious one. We often hear people describe themselves as "deeply spiritual, but not religious." While spirituality is accepted and even promoted, religion is denigrated, thought to be suspect or worse, the cause of inhuman acts. From our twenty-first-century vantage point, we have seen terrible things done in God's name: September 11, wars, genocide, persecutions, suicide bombings, terrorism, torture and oppression. A friend once told me, "Religion has lost it. Look at all the people killed and mutilated, and all because of religion."

Downey noticed a sharp line of separation drawn by many between spirituality and religion. He says:

> At the core of the American mindset is a sharp contrast between religion and spirituality, together with an implicit judgment that spirituality and the sacred are essential, while religion, perhaps helpful to some is not necessary to living a deeply spiritual life. In this view religion is incidental, and indeed may be an obstacle in walking the spiritual path. Spirituality is often understood as a very individual, personal, indeed private matter, whereas religion entails participation in the life of a community, in its worship, adhering to its norms and values.[6]

In order to attain greater integration and completeness we need to recognize our deeply felt personal desire for wholeness. If we are to persevere in our spiritual quest, we need more than we can bring to it ourselves alone. Downey claims that religious institutions mediate or communicate the experience of the sacred. Such mediation takes place through the "religious body's sacred texts, communal worship, traditions, social arrangements of leadership, authority, governance."[7] Right now there is a strong distrust of institutional authority, any authority, be it government, corporate or church. Indeed, the actions of many in these institutions including the church have earned distrust. If religion is seen as an untrustworthy institutional mediator of the sacred, it has indeed failed in the eyes of many.

Religion Requires Commitment

The problem with a "go it alone" spiritual quest is that it becomes in the words of the *Fortune* magazine editor, "deeply felt and deeply personal" but purely a private matter. However, as Downey points out, if the search for personal integration is a major constant in every spiritual quest, then adherence to religious beliefs, belonging to a religious tradition and affiliating with a religious community makes a lot of sense. When it comes to the deepest desires of the human heart, you are talking about something much more profound than an individual's personal tastes or pleasures.

Put another way, the problem for us in this quest is that more than feelings are required. Religion calls for commitment to others, to a collection of others in a tradition and to God who is beyond us all. It requires trust. To many today it seems very foolish to trust anyone or anything, even ourselves. As we search for the sacred, we come to learn that going it alone is inadequate in the long run.

Downey maintains that religion is much more than any one particular religious institution. It has three elements, all of which must be held together. The first is the institutional dimension where our quest for the sacred is formalized, structured, made concrete with traditions, texts, patterns of community and authority that mediate our sense of the sacred to us and facilitate our communion with the sacred. Second, there is the intellectual element of religion with formulations of cogent systems of thought and the development of our capacity for critical reflection to help us clarify our understanding of the sacred and communicate it to others. This intellectual element also serves our religious communities and us when the gift of the sacred is betrayed. The third element is the mystical element, the experience of the sacred.[8]

Religion does require commitment to a community of believers, to know and understand what that community stands for and to act out of concern for those values and beliefs. Spirituality, by comparison, is a free lunch. It does not cost energy or effort, anything like aligning oneself with a fallible collection of humans struggling within an institution.

While we have to recognize institutional shortcomings as well as our own, our initial visit with Peter in the High Priest's courtyard reminds us that our faith community has always been embedded in real life. Guided and empowered by the Holy Spirit, it is built upon the shoulders of fallible men and women who sometimes stumble and fall and then get up and do heroic things, as did the first followers of Jesus Christ. In the broadest sense, our spirituality is our way of living. Again, according to Michael Downey, "Christian spirituality is not one dimension of life. It *is* Christian life in the presence and by the power of the Holy Spirit, being conformed to the person of Christ and united in communion with God and others. Personal integration takes place and through conformity to the person of Christ."[9]

Following Christ should be reason enough to want to be united in common with God and others. It should be reason enough to want to stand on the shoulders of the fallible, yet faithful, men and women who went before us. It should be reason enough to accept responsibility to promote the good, achievable only through acts of faith, hope and charity. We should accept and relish the love of God poured into our hearts through the Holy Spirit.

Spirituality on the Job

We can experience the fire that burns within us. We know our constant need for the moral compass to help us stay on course. We recognize the thrill of a job well done. We have felt the wind at our backs carrying us through. More often than not, those experiences have come on the job.

Most of us will spend the majority of our waking hours as adults at work. Add to that the time spent preparing for our career in school and in training. Then, there is the time preparing for, traveling and worrying about work. We must also recognize the work we do for which we do not get paid. We spend well over half our entire lives working. At work, more than anywhere else, our lives play out. This is where we pour out our proverbial blood, sweat and tears. If we are to integrate our lives, if we are to realize our aspiration to move closer to God, it will have to be where we spend our days, and sometimes our nights and weekends as well. It is in our everyday lives, in our day-to-day experiences that God is drawing us to God's own self. The circumstances, events, problems and opportunities that we meet each day, the lives we live each day are where we encounter God. A spirituality of work begins with the recognition of this and that those we encounter are important agents on our path to self-transcendence toward a loving, inviting, empowering God.

God calls us where we are, in the ordinary, the humdrum, the drudgery of work as well as the thrilling, rewarding and eventful occasions we might experience on the job. Our spirituality must encompass the whole of our lives, our relationships with God and our neighbor as much as our interior lives of prayer and growing self-understanding. This means that the social, political and most certainly the economic realms—every dimension of our personal and communal lives—are in play in our journey toward the sacred, our journey to God.

Many would concede that their work takes up a good part of their lives and that they have experienced some growth and maturation while on the job, but they say it is a real stretch to think of the workplace as holy ground, a place where one might encounter God or we grow toward God. Holy places are supposed to be special, set aside, mysterious, awe-inspiring. Few can describe their work that way. Spiritual disciplines, prayer, fasting, asceticism, meditation, contemplation, worship all require time and space not available on the job. Spirituality and work require time, energy and effort. Even if we agree that who we are and what we do at work are important to our growth and development, important to our path toward wholeness, integrity and self-transcendence, how can we be seriously "spiritual" and still get our jobs done? How can we find God at work? This question will guide our considerations in the chapters that follow.

Exercise

1. Give thanks to God for the time to consider your work and your relationship with him.

2. Ask for the grace to seek God in your life at work as you go about your everyday affairs.

3. Think about your work. List five satisfying, exciting, wonderful things you can say about what you do and are able to do in

your work life. Write them down; look them over. What does your list say about your work and your desires?

4. Identify five things you find most troubling or discouraging about your work. Again, write them down, look them over. What do the things on this list say to you about your work and your own quest for integration of body, mind and soul?

5. Tell God about your findings, what you are going to do about it and what you want God's help with.

6. In gratitude, close with a prayer—your own or the Our Father.

CHAPTER 5

THE CORPORATE CULTURE

So far, we have been examining what is going on inside us, what drives us, and, to a degree, how we operate as persons and as Christians when we go about our work. As the stories and accounts thus far illustrate, when we go to work we are not isolated. We are a part of the world around us. We are embedded in a "corporate culture" and our organizations are themselves enmeshed in a wider business culture that is becoming more and more global in scope.

There are many critics of our culture who echo the recent complaint of a small-business operator at a Woodstock-sponsored conference on business and ethics. His telling observation, "It's a poisonous sea we swim in," summed up the feelings of many. Indeed, our culture seems to promote blindness, egoism, selfishness, inattention, amnesia and fearfulness or timidity. The world around us, of which we are a part, seems dead set on derailing our growth as Christians in the marketplace.

The late Pope John Paul II, a most articulate critic of the culture of selfishness that he saw dominating the Western world, observed in his message for the World Day of Peace, January 1, 2001:

> The authenticity of each human culture, the soundness of its underlying ethos, and hence the validity of its moral bearings, can be measured to an extent by its commitment *to the human cause* and by its capacity *to promote human dignity* at every level and in every circumstance.
>
> The radicalization of identity which makes cultures resistant to any beneficial influence from outside is worrying enough; but no less perilous is the slavish

> conformity of cultures, or at least of key aspects of them, to cultural models deriving from the Western world. Detached from their Christian origins, these models are often inspired by an approach to life marked by secularism and practical atheism and by patterns of radical individualism. This phenomenon of vast proportions, sustained by powerful media campaigns and designed to propagate lifestyles, social and economic programs and, in the last analysis, a comprehensive world-view which erodes from within other estimable cultures and civilizations. Western cultural models are enticing and alluring because of their remarkable scientific and technical cast, but regrettably there is a growing evidence of their deepening human, spiritual and moral impoverishment. The culture which procures such models is marked by the fatal attempt to secure the good of humanity, by eliminating God, the Supreme Good.[1]

Ours is a culture inspired by an approach to life marked by "secularism, practical atheism, and patterns of radical individualism." Our culture represents a "fatal attempt to secure the good of humanity, by eliminating God." Not a pretty picture. We can applaud our Western way of life as fostering freedom, liberty and the highest standards of living ever known to humankind. These achievements need to be weighed with the shortcomings that alarmed Pope John Paul II. Indeed, the pros and cons of this debate have raged on and on. It is a regular fixture of many Woodstock discussions. But what is important to people at work more than anything else is to be aware of the world in which they operate and to see how their particular business environment is affecting their own view of things, their decisions and actions.

Ethical Corporate Culture

The fact is that we do live in a post-Christian world where our culture can no longer be assumed to hold Judeo-Christian values. That is evident in all areas of life, most particularly in business and commerce. Many see this as a bad thing, while others recognize that we are called to the adult task of shouldering our values for ourselves as we live and work. In an effort to assess the impact of our business culture on us as well as our impact on it, we visit two stories. These are conversations from two Woodstock meetings where the culture of the business world played a significant role.

The first meeting explored the issue of what it takes to maintain an ethical corporate climate. As the conversation proceeded, the managing partner of a large law firm observed that good ethics and a good corporate culture come from the top:

> I find that it is the people at the top who are responsible for articulating, sustaining and commending a healthy culture that contributes to a good corporate culture. In my company there was an outstanding person who was also a senior partner in our law firm and a very good lawyer at that. He was very religious, and in the workplace he expressed his religion through his behavior, not by explicitly religious words. His principal contribution was in the transmission of the culture of this law firm.[2]

Another lawyer at that meeting agreed that values come from the top. He explained that courage is a core value for his firm:

> I believe it is up to our firm's leadership to communicate the values that constitute our culture. We bear this responsibility. This is particularly true in our orientation of new people into the firm. It is very important. What we regard as the litmus test for consistency with our culture is

> courage. Courage is equivalent to independent responsibility to make correct judgment in conflict situations. A courageous person is able to do the right thing even under stress and pressure. It's an independent obligation that the lawyer must exercise such as not to become captive to one's own client. The lawyer is a professional who is obliged to tell the truth to the client even though the client may not want to hear it.

The executive director of a large trade association jumped in at that point:

> I think most firms are very high on ethics internally, that is to say within their own company. They are quite content and even eager to treat employees fairly and well. But when it comes to outside competition, it is an altogether different story: In competition "anything goes," and ethics goes right out the window. It's a war, and whatever needs to be done to win the war is what the company will do.

With that observation the issue was joined. The first reaction was a question posed by a person who had long worked in the sale of computer and information technology systems to the federal government:

> I'm intrigued by this distinction between the internal and external culture of businesses, in which one treats one's competitors very differently than one treats employees. What accounts for this difference, and how can people live with such inconsistency?

The trade association executive responded:

> I think it is a simple question of pragmatism. A company talks itself into the need to wage warfare in a competitive way. If you need to mislead you mislead; anything goes in

> war, anything is fair. It's a rather schizophrenic duality.

That brought a sharp rejoinder from the information technology sales executive:

> I just don't buy that. I think it is terribly false to think of business as a model of warfare, and it is unrealistic to talk about a division between the inside ethical attitude and the outside warfare attitude. If a firm does not have a consistent corporate culture such that the inside and the outside are both concerned with honesty, ethics and treating people fairly, the firm simply won't last. When word gets out, whether to your competitors or your customers, that your ethical behavior is inconsistent—your fate is sealed. Inside and outside must go together, and they must be consistent.

The discussion surged back and forth. At the conclusion the group was asked to reflect on their conversations that day. How did they go? A senior federal government executive summarized his feelings, "I found today's session somewhat depressing in so far as we were dwelling on the absence of morality or ethics in the business culture. Perhaps, it was depressing because we were nudged beyond our comfort zone."

There are several things to notice about this first conversation. This was not an academic exercise. These conflicting observations about the culture of business itself came from the participants' experience in the workplace of their business cultures. The first saw that it is "like warfare out there," justifying an anything-goes attitude toward competitors that would not be accepted internally. This is consistent with the "poisonous sea" remark noted at the beginning of this chapter. By contrast, the lawyer whose firm valued courage, doing the right thing even under stress and pressure, may have the more optimistic view of the business environment. Yes, there are stressful, challenging and even contentious times. But no situation is far from impossible, and it is hardly necessary to discard the values of promoting honesty, ethics and treating people fairly. Realistically, it can be rough and at the same time a thrilling venue for accomplishing great good.

Our business environment can lead to ethical and virtuous practices when clear, courageous action is valued. On the other hand, it can defeat and marginalize good decisions and actions. We need to recognize the structures and the cultural and environmental elements that serve as barriers to our quest for integration and wholeness. We have to learn how to overcome and, where we can, restructure our work environment to promote the God-seeking quest of everyone. We also must affirm and promote those structures and business patterns that favor ethical business practices.

Notice, in this conversation, the general recognition that what goes on within an organization is frequently mirrored in its external actions. Thus the participants observed that a firm lacking a consistent, morally appropriate corporate culture will not last. Finally, notice the dynamic of the conversation itself. In this particular situation, people freely shared their observations. They supported and disagreed with each other, and challenged each other on important issues.

A Bad Business Decision and Christian Values

The second conversation features a discussion involving members of another Woodstock group who had just read an article from the *Harvard Business Review* called "The Hidden Traps in Decision Making" by John S. Hammond, Ralph L. Keeney and Howard Raiffa.[3] They checked business mistakes they had made against the several invisible traps mentioned in the article. They wanted to gain a better understanding about what went wrong.

The article's authors claimed that our minds develop shortcuts in order to process complex information quickly so that we can come to conclusions in complex situations. These shortcut habits are generally very helpful but can become "traps" that block good decisions. They argue that the best defense is to be aware of the possibility that a trap might be at work when making important decisions. Two of the pitfalls they identified came out during the discussion that day.

The authors called one the "anchoring trap." This is the very familiar situation when, in considering a decision, our minds give disproportional weight to the first information received. Initial impressions, estimates or data anchor subsequent thoughts and judgments. Another pitfall was called the "confirming evidence trap." Confirming evidence, or bias, leads us to favor information that supports our existing instinct or point of view while avoiding information that contradicts it.

There are two fundamental psychological forces at work here. The first is our tendency to subconsciously decide what we want to do before we figure out why we want to do it. The second is our inclination to be more engaged by things we like rather than by things we dislike.

One participant described what was, for him, one of his biggest business mistakes. He took his company that manufactured the fabrics used in clothing, linens, furnishings and floor coverings for home and office, into a new area. The company began to produce materials for sale to arts and crafts retailers. He felt it was a great idea. So he hired a major consulting firm to come in and analyze the situation and its potential before going forward.

The consulting firm provided a confirming report. They agreed that there was great potential in this new venture but said that his organization did not have the necessary expertise in-house to pull it off. He would have to hire someone from the outside to run it. He did that. He hired a woman (who up to that point in her career had shown great success) to a three-year contract; she was supposed to be a "wonder kid." It turned out that her performance on this particular project was less than desirable.

> The irony is that I had a nephew who was a young salesman for us. He said to me, "Look, she's a phony, and either she goes or I go." That was really putting me on the spot. We had her under a three-year contract and this was after the first six months. We kept her. He left and started his own business, which turned out to be highly successful doing exactly what we were trying to do.[4]

After the nephew left, this participant's company went through several managers and various marketing arrangements to try to salvage the operation. But it never showed a profit. He said, eventually, "I had to fire the 'wonder kid' because she was not producing. She was tough, had a strong personality, but nothing to show." He then sold off the operation.

He concluded that he bought into the consultants' advice because it confirmed his "great idea." He thought it would bring a flow of new revenue into the company. And because the consultants were well-regarded experts, he followed their advice, and hired the "wonder kid" and kept her on at the expense of his nephew. And, to top it off, he lost money. He concluded that he made a poor business decision, or series of poor decisions, that negatively affected his company financially. Both the "anchoring trap" and the "confirming evidence trap" caught him. Then he remarked that he did not see how Christian values had anything to do with the decisions he made.

At this point another participant, a friend who also headed his own company, broke in:

> Let me take your case and contradict you. The first thing I notice is, you're saying it was a pure business decision. That means that it impacted profits. For you, business equals questions of profit and loss. But we already agreed that there are a whole range of values involved in business, profits being just one of them.
>
> You decided that the nephew would have to go if he followed up on his ultimatum to you. He said, "If you don't fire this woman, I'll walk." Either you fired her or he walked. There are deep values involved here. There were deeply personal relationships that you had to weigh. Profitability was not the first thing facing you. There were loyalties; there was a contract; and there was the process you went through when you got into the new business. You've got family. You know the young man is smart, up and coming. You would have liked to have him stay in the business. Maybe he was going to be the future of your business. You are making a very personal decision here in which profit was not the priority.

The man agreed that he knew his nephew was good, but too young and inexperienced. The friend continued by identifying the Christian values that were evident to him in this story:

> I would read into your story that, at the time, you had a commitment to the woman you had hired and determined to honor that commitment. It was unfortunate that your nephew left. You called on your integrity here. You could have broken the contract.
>
> You also had a commitment to being rational, to go by the facts rather than on somebody else's hunch.
>
> The point I'm trying to drive at is you behaved in a way that was very fair-minded and very consistent with the facts known at the time. You were being reasonable, intelligent and responsible. This is thoroughly Christian.

Still, the man with the failed business venture said that he did not get how his story of mistaken judgments had anything to do with Christian values. He made mistakes in opening up this new venture, hiring the particular person to run the new operation and keeping her on at the expense of losing a promising potential successor. He lamented that he did not have all the facts at the time. Later on, he learned some things about her past business practices that would have kept him from hiring her in the first place.

The friend answered:

> I think sometimes we have to accept the fact that in the normal course of doing our jobs, we often take for granted that our judgments or decisions are in fact made in a Christian context. Look how you stood by your commitments and how you responded, intelligently and reasonably, both when you got started and again later when things did not work out. All of this you took for granted as you described your story. They are all part of being a good Christian person, someone who transacts business on the good side and the tough side. Implicit in the story was that you came to see that this woman was not exactly your type of person. Her values and behaviors were not like yours. That is bound to have been a factor in switching her out. All those are implicit ways that you were a good Christian person.
>
> These are Christian values. Your description could be a great example of how to stay on the right course, how not to cut and run, how not to take the easy way out because of pressure. There are a lot of things that you just took for granted as a part of your story that other people would applaud you for and make them want to work for your organization.

Notice how the conversation affirmed and supported the man who told his story. Again, the friend was free to challenge and affirm, free to point out what was obvious to him but was missed by the principal actor in the story. Here we see that a well-intentioned, values-driven businessperson can miss the role that his Christian values played in this important aspect of his life. Yet, the values were there at work for others to see. The decision to go into the new line of business cost him and his company, but his display of integrity and willingness to make the hard decision when the facts called for it probably would make many others want to work for his organization.

He did not have all the facts at the time of hiring or six months later when the nephew expressed his misgivings. We rarely, if ever, have all the facts. We know that we are not going to be perfect. Nevertheless, we are called to do as good a job as we can, wherever and whenever. We are not going to know everything but we can get closer by being aware and open. Christian values motivated this man to act with integrity, rationality and responsibility throughout the process. He had to admit his mistakes and move on to correct the situation.

The business world is tough and challenging, but it can be a place where Christian values animate what we do and how we do it. What we do, the judgments and decisions we make, may be formed by and carry Christian values. Just as we can avoid mistakes by awareness of the hidden traps that might block us, explicit awareness of our Christian values can inform our business decisions and actions. This can have a significant impact on our particular business culture and beyond.

In his letter to the International Union of Christian Business Executives (UNIAPAC) meeting in a Conference in Rome on March 5, 2004, Pope John Paul II spoke about this. He said in part:

> The financial and commercial sector is becoming increasingly aware of the need for sound ethical practices which ensure that business activity remains sensitive to its fundamentally human and social dimensions. Since the pursuit of profit is not the sole end of such activity, the Gospel challenges business men and women to embody respect both for the dignity and creativity of their employees and customers and the demands of the common good. On a personal level they are called to develop important virtues such as: "diligence, industriousness, prudence in undertaking reasonable risks, reliability and fidelity in interpersonal relationships, and courage in carrying out decisions which are difficult and painful" (*Centesimus Annus*, 32). In a world tempted by consumerist and materialist outlooks, Christian executives are called to affirm the priority of "being" over "having."[5]

In this chapter we have been examining business culture from the vantage point of people right in the middle of it. What does a business culture look like to people as they attempt to do the right thing each day? We have seen differing descriptions about what the business culture is like. Some people have said that it is "a poisonous sea" and that there is a "war out there." Others came to understand that business culture is somewhat more benign. And many found that it is a culture, when informed by Christian values, which rewards those who are diligent, industrious and prudent. We have also seen the importance of values such as integrity, acting rationally and responsibly, reliability and fidelity in interpersonal relationships, prudence in undertaking reasonable risks and courage in carrying out difficult and painful decisions. These values can become so embedded in individuals and in the cultures of the business they serve that one can overlook the fact that they are Christian values.

Exercise

For this exercise take a look at your own workplace and its corporate culture. What is culture, anyway? Bernard Lonergan, an important twentieth-century Jesuit theologian and philosopher, said, "A culture is a set of meanings and values informing [that is, giving form to] a common way of life, and there are as many cultures as there are distinct sets of such meanings and values."[6]

On the other hand, Archbishop Derek Worlock of Liverpool, England, is quoted as saying, "Culture is simply 'the way we do things around here.'"[7]

1. Give thanks to God for the time to consider things about your workplace culture that you might have overlooked. Ask for the grace to see your work situation for what it is in your life and to see how you influence it as you go about your everyday affairs.

2. Read 1 Corinthians 13:1–13. It is a familiar chapter. Read it aloud whether or not you are in a group, and read it slowly. Ponder the verses quietly for a time.

3. How would you describe the shared meanings and values that set the tone in your present work situation? How would you tell others about the "way we do things around here"? Remember the lawyer who spoke about courage as a defining value in his firm. Or is yours a "poisonous sea"?

4. Recall concrete instances where you felt blocked or limited by the culture of your workplace. Do you remember the feelings that accompanied that experience? What did you do in response?

5. What are some of the ways you can promote Christian values within your culture at work?

6. Tell God what you learned and what you would like to do to follow up. Ask for the grace to keep at it. Conclude with a prayer to carry out your resolve:

> *Loving God, give me the strength I need to carry out my resolve.*
> *Learning from your Gospel, grant me a spirit of deep and generous Christian devotion.*
> *Help me to promote your will and your glory, at work and in all I do. Amen.*

CHAPTER 6

CONTRIBUTE TO THE SANCTIFICATION OF THE WORLD

With all that goes into our makeup as persons and with the mix of shared meanings and values that animate our workplace cultures, one might still ask, "Is it possible to lead an ethical and moral life in business?" The stories recounted thus far and your own reflections should show that it is not only possible but also realistic to conclude that we can and do strive to lead ethical and moral lives, although it is not easy. With our noses to the grindstone and our habits long established, we might not even be aware that it is a life of Christian virtue we are leading. Based on our own experience and that of others at work, we can affirm that we are imperfect God-seekers who by God's grace can grow to choose wisely and rightly at work in the decisions we make, the actions we take and the people we become.

We have to recognize the sea we are swimming in for what it is. Do our workplace and our industry support ethical practices or put up roadblocks? We have to learn to recognize the structures and the cultural and environmental elements that serve as barriers to our quest for God. We have to identify and promote those structures, values and habits in our business culture that promote ethical business practices. Remember how the virtue of courage was identified and supported by the law firm in the last chapter. We must learn how to overcome barriers and hidden traps. We may need to restructure our work environment to promote God-seeking for all.

In his message to the Christian business leaders in March 2004, Pope John Paul II reminded those meeting in Rome and us that:

> Christian business leaders...bear witness to the values of God's Kingdom in the world of commerce. Their work is

> in fact rooted in that dominion and stewardship which God has given man over the earth (cf. Genesis 1:27) and finds particular expression in the promotion of creative economic initiatives with enormous potential to benefit others and to raise their material standard of living. Because "there is no human activity—even in secular affairs—which can be withdrawn from God's dominion (*Lumen gentium*, 36), Christians charged with responsibility in the business world are challenged to combine the legitimate pursuit of profit with a deeper concern for the spread of solidarity and the elimination of the scourge of poverty which continues to afflict so many members of the human family.[1]

It is one thing to respond to the fire burning within us and want to stop the compartmentalizing of our faith. It is one thing to come to realize that we cannot put our spiritual lives "on one side and the rest of our lives on the other side," as the Woodstock participant said in chapter four. That fire burning inside us might indeed motivate us to look beyond ourselves to recognize and accept the more daunting task of seeking to influence our organizations so that they can develop ethical and moral corporate cultures that are consistent with Christian values. But now we are told that as Christians in the world of work we are called by God to contribute to the sanctification of the world. This is a heavy-duty assignment. This is the mission to build the kingdom of Christ. The pope's observation reiterates an important teaching of the church found in the Second Vatican Council's Dogmatic Constitution on the Church, *Lumen gentium*, that it is the job of people in the workplace and elsewhere in the world "[T]o illuminate and order all temporal things with which they are so closely associated that these may be effected and grow according to Christ and may be to the glory of the Creator and Redeemer."[2]

Later on in *Lumen gentium*'s chapter on the laity, the church Fathers affirmed that as we work together at our jobs, businesses, professions, trades and callings, our "secular activity," we help each other to:

> [A]chieve greater holiness of life, so that the world may be filled with the spirit of Christ and may the more effectively attain its destiny in justice, in love and in peace. The laity enjoy a principal role in the universal fulfillment of this task. Therefore, by their competence in secular disciplines and by their activity, interiorly raised by grace, let them work earnestly in order that created goods through human labor, technical skill and civil culture may serve the utility of all men according to the plan of the creator and the light of his word.[3]

This is extremely challenging. How can we, in our ordinary work lives, help the world to more effectively attain its destiny in justice, in love and in peace? This task for laymen and laywomen to achieve greater holiness in life is really something new. Or is it? For most of our lives we have been praying the Lord's Prayer. We pray, "Thy kingdom come." Do we know what we are asking for? When we pray for the coming of the kingdom, we are praying that our world will be filled with the Spirit of Christ and will attain its destiny in justice, in love and in peace. We pray for the grace that we will carry out our responsibilities to spread the kingdom of Christ.

We want to know and do the right thing at work. And we want our work situations and our culture to help us and others to do the right thing. What the church fathers declared, and what John Paul II reaffirmed, is that by paying attention to those desires (the fire that burns within us) and developing important work virtues such as diligence, industriousness, prudence in undertaking reasonable risks, reliability and fidelity in interpersonal relationships and courage in carrying out decisions, we can help the world get closer to the ultimate virtues of justice, peace and love. We can come nearer to what we have been praying for all these years.

Woodstock groups periodically take up the question of structuring their business enterprises to be more consistent with Judeo-Christian values. What does that mean? How can it be done realistically? What is at risk in the attempt? They consider a variety of related questions. Once a meeting began with a reading from the prophet Amos, one that links socially just behavior with faith in and worship of God.

> Thus says the LORD:
> For three transgressions of Israel,
> and for four, I will not revoke the punishment;
> because they sell the righteous for silver,
> and the needy for a pair of sandals—
> they who trample the head of the poor into the dust of the earth,
> and push the afflicted out of the way;
> son and father go in to the same girl,
> so that my holy name is profaned;
> they lay themselves down beside every altar
> on garments taken in pledge;
> and in the house of their God they drink
> wine with fines they imposed.
>
> Yet I destroyed the Amorite before them,
> whose height was like the height of cedars,
> and who was strong as oaks.
> I destroyed his fruit above,
> and his roots beneath.
> Also I who brought you up out of the land of Egypt,
> and led you forty years in the wilderness,

to possess the land of the Amorite.
And I raised up some of your children to be prophets
and some of your youths to be nazirites.
Is this not indeed so, O people of Israel?
says the LORD. (Amos 2:6–11)

The passage provoked an array of spirited reactions that set the stage for the discussion that followed:

> I am tempted to say about the passage: "What else is new?" The problems and the suffering of the poor among us are age-old, and are with us today. I do think, however, that personally and institutionally we recognize the needs of the poor more clearly today than was the case in days gone by. So, some progress has been made. We are not generally motivated to harm the poor. Rather, we often just don't pay attention to them.[4]

That reaction was followed by the comments of a retired career military officer who now runs a manufacturing business. He said:

> This Scripture passage reminds me that I am being called to be a disciple of Christ and am being held to greater account than are those who don't believe. There are rights and wrongs and values. I know that; and, in a way it troubles me. I think about my own profession. I was in a profession where I had to kill people, and I had to come to grips with that. To do so, I went to the just war theory and so on. Later, I had to come to grips with other justice issues, such as, "What is just business practice?" And then, "What is just societal practice?" We all have to be responsible for all of this.[5]

Then the members of the group told about their experiences of being with others in the workplace and the communal dimensions of their work situations. They focused on what they thought was right and wrong, and how that played out in the context of where they worked and the people they worked with—those who reported to them, peers and superiors.

They remembered the striking discussion at a meeting several months before where layoffs and plant closings became the topic. The first to speak that day was a CEO who rushed into the meeting, looking a bit harried. He said that he had just flown in from a business trip and had not planned to attend. However, he felt he had to report back because of a discussion the group had earlier about loyalty at work. As he explained that he had just visited his company's facilities in the Midwest where he had gone to announce the decision to close those plants, all heads turned. Shutting down those operations ended up as the only viable solution. His company had failed to find any interested buyers or any other workable options. "We had to stop the bleeding."

Given the bleak financial assessment, he and his top management personnel felt they had no other choice. Nonetheless, he was troubled. He spoke of the wrenching decision-making process and the impact of the conversation about loyalty at the earlier meeting. He concluded that he personally had to break the news to the employees. Most CEOs would have sent out a memo on a Friday afternoon or put their human resources manager on a plane. But he did not take that path. He explained:

> I think of the manager who was on the scene when we closed the plants. He knows all the families of all these workers. You have multiple responsibilities: inside the organization and outside to the larger community. We discussed all of this. I made the decision, and I'm convinced it was the right thing to do. I had to look my people in the eye and tell them why.[6]

He had told the group that he was determined to carry out the closings in the most humane way possible. He made sure the employees were given extended medical benefits, and he hired an outplacement firm to help them find new jobs. Where possible, the company absorbed the laid-off people elsewhere within the organization.

Reflecting on what happened, he observed that decisions have to be made every day and that sometimes what we do hurts people. The real question for the CEO was: What was his responsibility to his employees as a Christian? He saw several options. One was to duck the hard decision and let someone else deal with the continuing losses later. The other was to accept responsibility, close the plant and confront the employees himself. For him, making these decisions, although personally difficult, were the right things to do and, he believed, part of his Christian responsibility.

With that earlier discussion very much in mind, a manager from a local media company picked up on the theme of Christian responsibility noting that as a boy in a Catholic grade school he used to think he had a vocation to become a priest.

> It was only in the last few years that it has occurred to me that I do have a vocation, and I was reminded of it again in the conversation we've been having about the plant closing. There have been times in my life when I, too, have had to terminate employees or to do something that has an adverse impact on a lot of people. But I think our primary emphasis is rather on the constructive side—on the opportunity that we have to affect people in a positive way.
>
> Even though your action may be painful now, if you are doing the right thing you must realize that you simply do not know what God's plan is for those people that you lay off. So, even in the pain and confusion of taking an

> action like that, I think you have to realize that it's a great privilege to serve a lot of people. I haven't focused really on that until very recently.[7]

"You're right," another added. "We all have had the opportunity to act as Christians, even in things that are very difficult to do." He continued, "As I see it, there is always going to be someone on your team who is going to propose an unethical way to get the job done. What is your responsibility in that case? The answer is pretty obvious. I hope we will say to such a person, 'Let's see if we can get it done, but let's do it the right way.'"

An executive with a contracting firm picked up the discussion. He argued:

> I also think we have to look for proactive ways of dealing with people. The other night we had a meeting about a construction job. One person can set the tone of a meeting like that simply by the way in which he speaks, the language he uses, the signals he gives off and so forth. One person can lead the group into thinking unethically or ethically. And all of a sudden other people will simply say, "Yeah, we'll do that," or, "We don't need to do that." That's why I think that part of our vocation is setting the focus in a positive way and drawing the very best out of people.

And a senior partner with a major firm confessed:

> I've been embarrassed at times because I did not pick up on an ethical issue before somebody else did. And oftentimes that somebody else was from another religious tradition. It has been my experience, for example, that other people often pick up the moral and ethical issues very quickly and articulate them very well. And I have to say to myself, "That's right. I should have thought of that."

As the meeting was about to conclude, a man in the financial services profession reflected on the various questions that had been addressed and concluded:

> All of this makes me more aware that there are dimensions to my business and to my responsibilities to the business community that go beyond the transaction at hand and simply winning. My job is not simply the way I earn my living. There are times when I've done things that are technically and legally right, but I haven't felt good about them. I think that was my conscience telling me that I really need to go beyond all of that and look at the more I should have done.

What we see in these conversations is that the business virtues John Paul II called for are developing in the participants as they grapple with the situations at work. The story of the plant closings demonstrated diligence, prudence, reliability and fidelity on the part of the CEO involved. He spoke about the courage necessary to make and carry out a tough decision and personally demonstrated that courage as he delivered and explained the bad news. He showed concern for those affected and matched that concern with actions that lessened the blow. Group members took that lesson to heart as they continued to grow in their vocations at work.

It is a fact that at any given juncture someone on your team at work may propose an unethical way to get the job done. Here, the participants recognized their responsibility to set the tone. "Setting the focus in a positive way" and "drawing out the best" in people is part of our vocation, they affirmed. They also recognized that because of the press of time in any given situation they might miss an important ethical issue that others will pick up right away. This calls for two other business virtues: openness and humility.

We also see the insights and encouragement at the meetings help the participants to grow in their responses to the Spirit as they address the questions about just business practices and just societal practices. With small, discrete, concrete actions and attitudes, they are helping the world attain its destiny in justice, peace and love. They are bearing witness to Christ's kingdom in commerce.

Exercise

1. Give thanks to God for the time to consider your work as a reflection of the creative action of God himself and ask for the grace to see God's hand in your work situation.

2. Reread the passage from Matthew's Gospel about Joseph obeying God's instructions to take the "child and his mother" to Egypt and then to return to the land of Israel after Herod's death (Matthew 2:13–15, 19–23).

3. No human activity has been withdrawn from God's dominion. Is it possible to see your work as having a role in bringing about the kingdom of God?

4. Has your work been an occasion to develop the important business virtues mentioned by Pope John Paul II such as diligence, industriousness, prudence in undertaking reasonable risks, reliability and fidelity in interpersonal relationships, and courage?

5. Can you set a tone so that ethical issues, respect for the dignity and creativity of coworkers and customers and demands of the common good are considered along with making a profit?

6. Pause and review your answers and anything that struck your heart as you considered these questions. Have you decided to do anything as a result?

7. Pray for the grace to carry out your resolve and that the kingdom of justice, love and peace will come. Say the Our Father.

CHAPTER 7
A FIVE-POINT PROGRAM FOR DOING THE RIGHT THING IN BUSINESS

Business ethics is a very practical form of working out who we are in the company of our fellow creatures at work. We have to learn who we are while embroiled in a business culture that is sometimes quite challenging and difficult. As we have seen it can be a poisonous sea we swim in and a war zone where survival is the watchword and anything goes. It can also be a challenge that is fun and exciting.

We have heard the voices of men and women coming out of their situations at work, getting their jobs done and manifesting Christian virtues in the process. Sometimes they did not even realize that what they did showed Christian virtues until others pointed this out. Easy for them, we might say. Maybe they are somehow special. But what about the rest of us? We make mistakes, fall short and often have a lot less control over our work situation. How can we work out who we are and do the right thing when there are demands for productivity, profitability and the need to anticipate and respond in the face of constant change? Indeed, it seems that the one constant is change: technological, social and cultural. We find ourselves in a world of flux and upheaval.

How do we do the right thing and integrate mind, body and soul in a world of business characterized by heavy demands and constant change? How do we lead a spiritual life at work? How do we shape and carry the fire within us to do the right thing? What are the disciplines and habits that can help us to channel the drive, desire, dynamism within us to reach greater integration and completeness and contribute to the sanctification of the world?

The Emergence of a Five-Point Program

From years of rich Woodstock Business Conference conversations, we can distill the essential elements that together form a firm foundation for doing the right thing in business. They are tested by the lived experience of men and women on the job.

To set the stage and illustrate how the wisdom emerges from these discussions, let us drop in on one of many Woodstock meetings across the country where participants considered the question: How do Christian values affect how we deal with problems in an area of chaos? The Scripture passage chosen for the meeting focused on Jesus' words about the impossibility of serving two masters and what we should and should not be worrying about (Matthew 6:24–43). Tom Peters's book *Thriving on Chaos* served as background reading. Peters claimed in this book that a business leader's vision had to be both specific enough to act as a tiebreaker and general enough to leave room for the bold initiatives required for survival in a "chaotic" business environment.

During the discussion that day the term "tiebreaker" became shorthand for the collection of values that pushes us in one direction or another on moral questions. The question for the group was how to make one's Christian values the "tiebreaker." When making critical decisions, how do we make sure that our Christian values play a significant role in the decision-making and action-implementing process? In the course of the conversation, participants explored their own core values as they grappled with the tiebreaker question. The meeting began with the observation:

> What I think we are trying to do tonight is to go through this to find out what our core values are or should be in business. What are the core ways of doing business that will give us the tools to move forward in a world that is essentially in chaos? Or, at least it is a world that moves a lot faster today than it did twenty, thirty, forty years ago.[1]

Another, whose software company had been dealing with the difficult problem of layoffs and office closings, joined in:

> I think all of us who have made business decisions know that the question is: How do you bring Christian values into the tiebreaker? The toughest equations are situations when the business exigency is for quick action. It may be layoffs. It may be that the quick action is necessary when the Christian value would call for a little more patience, a little charity. How do you draw the line in those kinds of cases? A lot of companies have come to a bad end and have hurt hundreds of thousands of people by going bankrupt and out of business. The operating facilities close, and people lose their jobs because the company didn't cut their costs early enough. I think it's not an easy decision when you have to worry about firing a person. Sometimes the best thing to do is fire him or her and, while it hurts the individual and the immediate family, it keeps the company alive and there are thousands of others that you save that way. So, I don't think one can always approach tiebreakers on the ground that, "We have to be nice to the fellows immediately involved." You have to think of all of the people involved.

On this point there was general agreement, even from those who had recently been on the wrong end of a corporate downsizing exercise.

Taking into account of the legitimate interests of all takes time to sort out. It also requires the ability to reflect on and have the big picture in mind. These decisions not only involve whether or not to take a direction or action but also how to do it. At each juncture Christian values can play an important role in the outcome, but it is not always easy.

A note of realism was added toward the end of the meeting:

> If you're running a business in a capitalist society, there are all kinds of different and sometimes conflicting forces. Only some of them are what I consider Christian values. It seems to me that it's a constant struggle to see to it that those dangerous or harmful tendencies of society are resisted and, if possible, humanized. I think we are kidding ourselves when we allow a competitive, innovative society to impose anti-Christian tendencies. Not because making a profit is wrong, but because the things people can do in blind pursuit of profit or power can be extremely unchristian.

To top off the difficulties noted so far, even the most benevolent and visionary businessperson has to deal with the fast pace of things. As the conversation continued, one participant asked:

> How do Christian values affect how we deal with all these problems when it looks like chaos all around? It seems all of us have more things to do each day than we can possibly do. I stop working at 11 P.M. at night and I still haven't finished the day's work. Some of us just can't do everything that's on our plates. How do we bring Christian values to bear on the choices we make about what work we should do out of all the things we're *supposed* to do, but don't have time for?

The first answer came from a very busy man who had just flown back from a day trip to New York. He travels four or five days a week:

> You're running every instant of the day—to a meeting, to a phone call, to an airplane, etc. How, in that kind of environment, do you align yourself from time to time with

> what you're supposed to be doing? I'll tell you, a friend of mine carries around a Prayer of Saint Francis card. He gave me the prayer too, and told me to pull it out and read it every once in a while. He told me to just think about the prayer and not about the next meeting I would be dashing off to. He gave me two other prayers, as well, the Hail Mary and the Act of Contrition. He advised me to read these during the day, too. He explained that it would keep me from thinking too highly of myself and from being too preoccupied with my business.

Another member, a Jesuit priest and a former university president, said that the last comment triggered something in him:

> The Jesuits were founded by Ignatius of Loyola. He used some "funny" terminology for things, and one of those funny words was *Examen*. Ignatius wanted his men to pause each day in a contemplative way, to give thanks to God and then ask for God's light. It is a regular exercise intended to make us more aware. It is an examination of consciousness. You become aware during the day of how much God's grace has touched you. This awareness is grace. The Examen gives you a chance to pause and say, "How am I doing?" Then, finally, the prayer ends by consciously applying that grace to your life. It opens you up to further grace or success as you move on with life. It is really an examination of how conscious and aware you are of how God has touched you and the graces you've had during the day. Sure, you might have some regrets that you haven't done as well as you might, but looking forward positively, you might do better. (See Appendix 2 for a form of the Ignatian Examen, crafted by Father Martin O'Malley, S.J., for business and professional men and women who are trying to do the right thing, seeking wholeness and integrity.)

These excerpts from one of the many productive Woodstock Business Conference conversations illustrate how the critical elements for a five-point program for wholeness and integrity emerge. From this one meeting we see the necessity of self-awareness, community and prayer. The conversation showed individuals expanding their horizons and engaging, bringing their faith-formed values to the workplace. Here all agreed that we have to be aware of, remember and rely upon the core values that transcend particular situations: values of respect for the dignity of all and concern for the good of the common enterprise were highlighted. Participants expanded what they had been aware of and concerned about. They had to recognize respect for individuals and honor concern for the good of the enterprise, even where they were in tension. The conversation demonstrated a community at work, encouraging and supporting its members as they labored to harmonize these central values. Encouragement came from the witness of a respected member who had to make hard choices and from the empathetic understanding of people who'd had similar experiences. A part of the peer support underscored the value of prayer and reflection. Specific prayers were offered as examples.

As the meeting concluded, one of the members remarked: "As we said earlier, a lot of this comes down to concern for the particular people. In the midst of the chaos, you have to be respectful of the dignity of the people, even those who are shouting at you and making all kinds of demands."

The Five-Point Program

Borrowing from Ronald Rolheiser, O.M.I., Chris Lowney, author of *Heroic Leadership*,[2] and many Woodstock Business Conference members, I would like to offer this five-point program for wholeness and integrity to develop and nourish the foundation we need for doing the right thing at work.

1. Self-awareness
2. Expanding our horizon, what we are aware of and concerned about, to include concern for all in God's creation
3. Engagement in our work and our world
4. Community
5. Prayer

There is no order of preference here. Each element is essential. When each is attended to, healthy growth results. The Woodstock stories demonstrate that ethical actions as well as the actors' mature development and personal integration are products of this five-point program.

In *The Holy Longing*, Father Rolheiser's book on spirituality, he identifies four nonnegotiable pillars for Christian spirituality, and all four are necessary for a healthy program of integrity and completeness. Rolheiser says, "Jesus was prescribing four things as an essential praxis for a healthy spiritual life: (a) private prayer and private morality; (b) social justice; (c) mellowness of heart and spirit; and, (d) community as a constitutive element of true worship."[3]

Chris Lowney's book on management and excellence in leadership, *Heroic Leadership*, examines the history of the Society of Jesus, the Jesuits, to find out what were the best practices to be gleaned from the successes and longevity of the "450-year-old company that changed the world." Those best practices, he suggests, can be applied generally and can help all in business find the right thing to do. His four pillars of leadership are:

- Self-awareness: understanding one's strengths, weaknesses, values and worldview,
- Ingenuity: confidently innovating and adapting to embrace a changing world,

- Love: engaging others with a positive, loving attitude, and
- Heroism: energizing self and others through heroic ambitions.[4]

While one author's concern is spirituality and the other's is organizational leadership, the overlap is obvious. Our program of five points merges the wisdom of these two thinkers with the practical, down-to-earth insights of Woodstock Business Conference participants.

Self-Awareness

One Woodstock regular, a retired Army general, put it this way when he recalled his thinking on being nominated by the President to be Chief of Staff of the Army. "I had to take stock and determine what my moral nonnegotiables were. I had to identify my core values and decide what orders I might be given that I possibly could not follow and would force me to resign." This Army general had to identify and name his nonnegotiables; we have to as well. As Lowney points out, "Leaders thrive by understanding who they are and what they value, by becoming aware of unhealthy blind spots or weaknesses that can derail them, and by cultivating the habit of continuous self-reflection and learning."[5]

Lowney marvels at the array of tools and practices the Jesuits invented, adopted and employed to mold self-awareness in their members. The tools included an extended retreat engaging in Ignatius of Loyola's *Spiritual Exercises,* tough manual labor, begging for food and lodging on a long pilgrimage, a weeklong retreat each year, and the *Examen*, described earlier, each day. Note that Saint Ignatius himself specifically recognized that few people engaged in business or public affairs can afford the time away for a thirty-day retreat. So he made provision for his exercises to be offered in everyday life to those who commit to pray a fixed period each day. The Ignatian Retreat in Daily Life (so-called Annotation 19 Retreat) enjoys wide and growing popularity today.

The self-awareness recommended here is not idle navel-gazing or self-absorbed narcissism. We begin by acknowledging who we are, unique creatures of God, born for a role in God's plan for his creation. The Psalmist, long ago, recognized this:

> O LORD, you have searched me and known me.
> You know when I sit down and when I rise up;
>   you discern my thoughts from far away.
> You search out my path and my lying down,
>   and are acquainted with all my ways.
> Even before a word is on my tongue,
>   O LORD, you know it completely.
> You hem me in, behind and before,
>   and lay your hand upon me.
> * * *
> For it was you who formed my inward parts;
>   you knit me together in my mother's womb.
> I praise you, for I am fearfully and wonderfully made.
>   Wonderful are your works;
> that I know very well. (Psalm 139:1–5, 13–14)

Our lives are a cooperative venture with God. Or, at the least, we hope to cooperate with God's plan for us. We are indeed, fearfully and wonderfully made. Our path to integration and wholeness requires that we try to understand ourselves as God's unique creations. Wonderful are God's works.

The data for understanding are right here in our lives. The challenge is finding the time and, perhaps, the guidance to plumb that experience. We need to know and appreciate our strengths; to understand and seek to improve where we find weaknesses; to discover and affirm our values, as the general did; and, to recognize the breadth and limits of our worldview, the things, people, ideals that we love and care about. This is an ongoing process. That is why the daily and other periodic checks and evaluations are so important.

Exercise

The goal of this exercise is to assess your own state of self-awareness. The assessment should be done privately. The results of the assessment, however, can be rich material for group discussion.

1. For this exercise, withdraw from the hubbub and chaos of work for a while. In your imagination step apart from yourself and look at yourself. Using your imagination, you may want to take a friend or companion with you who can help give you the necessary distance. In my case, I found Saint Joseph to be a great friend. He is a man depicted with his sleeves rolled up and the tools of his trade in his hands. He had a job from God of raising and training our Lord and protecting and supporting his wife, Mary. For me in the process of uncovering the truth, here is someone one can count on to see that things are right. God counted on him; so do I.

2. After finding the time and a place of peace, ask for God's guidance and insight.

3. Slowly read and pray over Psalm 139. Stop at something that touches you, moves you.

4. Invite the Holy Spirit (and your friend) to help you take inventory of your:

- Strengths—remember that you are fearfully, wonderfully made for God.
- Weaknesses—acknowledge them.

- Values—name your moral nonnegotiables.
- Worldview—what do you love and care about?

5. As you go through the inventory, make note of the things for which you are grateful as well as any weaknesses you would like to address.

6. Give thanks to God (and your companion) and say:

The Prayer of Saint Francis of Assisi
Lord, make me an instrument of your peace.
Where there is hatred, let me sow love;
Where there is injury, pardon;
Where there is doubt, faith;
Where there is despair, hope;
Where there is darkness, light;
Where there is sadness, joy.
O, Divine Master, grant that I may not so much seek
to be consoled, as to console;
To be understood as to understand;
To be loved as to love.
For it is in giving that we receive;
It is in pardoning that we are pardoned;
And it is in dying that we are born to eternal life.
Amen.

CHAPTER 8

EXPANDING OUR HORIZONS

We Have to Try to See with Jesus' Eyes

Scandals like Enron, Tyco, HealthSouth, Adelphia and WorldCom have provoked a flood of new legislation and regulations to force changes in the way corporations are governed and managed. Richard Thornburgh, former Pennsylvania governor and U.S. Attorney General who served as court-appointed examiner in the WorldCom bankruptcy, had a different take on what would force change in corporate America. Thornburgh gave his analysis at a Forum on Corporate Governance at Georgetown University that was sponsored by the Woodstock Theological Center and Georgetown University Law School in October 2004. "The real challenge," he said, "is to change the culture of corporate America." To this end he was optimistic that the lessons from WorldCom and the other scandals would end up empowering the "good guys." Those good guys are "members of management who are willing to be more transparent: auditors who will challenge suspect accounting schemes and corporate lawyers who will give unvarnished advice on questionable transactions." Thornburgh stressed his belief that a corporate culture that emphasizes ethical conduct will make more of a difference in the way corporations behave in the future than in any new regulations or laws.

The same forum featured Thomas Saporito, Ph.D., Senior Vice President of RHR International, a management consulting firm. He specializes in assisting CEOs and boards of directors with questions of governance, succession and recruitment. Doctor Saporito stressed that the solution to the problem rested with the boards of corporations exercising their responsibilities in the selection and monitoring of their CEOs and other top executives. Traditionally, boards of directors had three major responsibilities: the fiduciary responsibility to their shareholders, oversight of corporate strategies and the handling of succession from one CEO to the next. "Upholding the moral and ethical values of the company," he observed, has become another prime responsibility as the result of "the fall-out from the recent corporate scandals." When asked to assess a candidate for an executive or board position, he said, "There are two things I always look carefully at: a person's insight into himself or herself and the individual's motivational makeup—what their moral compass is."

The five-point program begins with self-awareness not just for the good of the individual but also as these experts in the area of corporate governance attest, for the good of our business organizations, our economic life and our society. We do not gain needed insight into ourselves in isolation. Nor is our "motivational makeup," our moral compass, an abstract ideal. We never operate in a vacuum, morally or otherwise. All that we do, including our moral decisions and actions, take place within a frame of reference or "horizon."

That frame of reference encompasses all that we know and care about, the people, events, ideas, worldview and assumptions about life that guide us in what we look for and see, what we understand and can explain, what we value and desire. We are limited to that horizon in what we can understand and appreciate at any particular time. What we know and care about determines what we are attracted to and what we try to avoid, day in and day out.

Once again this is illustrated in the discussion at a Woodstock Business Conference meeting. Participants began the day considering the rich man who was "dressed in purple and fine linen" in Luke 16:19–31 who never knew or cared about Lazarus, the poor man "covered with sores" who lay at his gate day after day. "He was invisible to the rich man," one Woodstock member pointed out after the passage was read. The topic for that day, "What it means to be living as a relatively wealthy person in business where many are poor," resulted from an observation made the previous month that there are many in our society who no longer count economically. There is little demand for uneducated brute labor. Machines and technology can accomplish work so much more efficiently. Those who in the past supplied that labor and worked their way up the ladder now have nowhere to go. And they, in turn, have become invisible to many.

Members conceded that many people do get overlooked because their ability to contribute economically is so limited. But ignoring people who no longer count economically is extremely troublesome. A management recruiter offered an initial take on the issue:

> The problem has two parts. The first is simple: If we're Christians, then we have a duty to do something about the problems of the people who "no longer count," the uneducated, and so forth. You can't avert your eyes from this suffering, because everyone is a child of God. This conclusion is inescapable. The second part of the problem is much more difficult: No one really understands the problem. It's extremely complex. How do you help these human beings, who constitute a very diverse group?[1]

The next to speak told a story about what happened to him when a poor man he encountered burst into the frame of his awareness one busy day:

> It is very important to know the situation of the people we are talking about. Jesus challenged the rigorous enforcement of purity laws that were used to define members and exclude nonmembers from the group.

> Jesus reached out to the outcasts; he valued them. Today, the disenfranchised supposedly have "no value" because they don't fit into the dominant motif of our age, which is business.
>
> A few days ago, I saw fear in the eyes of someone asking me for food. In that moment, I was able to see him as Jesus did. I put aside my "business values" (competition, productivity and profit) and saw that he was like me—made in the image and likeness of God. We have to try to see with Jesus' eyes.

A third participant reflected on her recent experience at a legal clinic and encouraged the group to expand their ideas about who might be overlooked by those fortunate enough to hold down good jobs and enjoy secure family situations. She told the group:

> There are two commandments, and both are simple: love God and love your neighbor.
>
> We should be wary of using the terminology "those people" when we talk about people who fall under the radar screen. We are not dealing with a problem that belongs exclusively to the uneducated and obviously disenfranchised. I saw a woman executive recently who got ill and lost her job; and was trying to avoid losing her house. I've seen many like her, managerial-level people coming to the legal services clinic because they've been laid off due to downsizing and so on.
>
> For ourselves, we want to avoid divorcing our personal and work lives. We need to get to know what is going on with people around us, whether or not we have handy solutions to the problem.

The conversation then moved to a discussion of potential solutions, with many varying suggestions offered, including government programs, voluntary activities, corporate initiatives and individual acts to address the problem. When the meeting ended it was clear to all concerned that with the story of Lazarus in the back of their minds, their eyes had been opened and their horizons (what they knew and cared about) had been expanded.

Actually most of what we know about the world comes from other people (parents, other family, neighbors, teachers, friends, mentors, books, popular media). Over time each of us constructs his or her own view of the world. According to former Woodstock Fellow, J. Michael Stebbins, Ph.D., that world, "my" world, is the sum of all I know, experience, care about and am interested in. It is not the world in its entirety; rather, it is the world as each of us knows it and lives it. Our world is limited. Anything outside is not a part of our world. What makes up "my" world can and does change over time. If I learn or experience more, my horizons and what I care about expand. Over time, we want our worlds, our horizons, to embrace more and more of the world that really is, God's creation.[2]

The Woodstock participants that day saw that they, like the rich man, recognized a tendency to overlook those in the community who were of little or seemingly no economic value. Because their horizons had been formed with Christian values, they recognized this as a problem. They found their model for recognizing the importance of the situation. They needed "to see with Jesus' eyes."

Social Justice

We are always going to be limited and will never see the whole of creation the way our Lord does. But the fire within us is propelling us to expand our horizons to take in more and more of the world, its beauties and its problems. It is the Holy Spirit calling us to gratitude and mobilizing us to be part of the solution. In his first sermons, Jesus told people to repent and embrace God's reign, the kingdom of God, which was at hand. What does that mean for us today?

For us to be able to embrace God's reign, our horizons have to expand to include those we tend to overlook or disregard and to recognize how our cultural and social systems affect us, both for good and for bad. It is not enough simply to be good within our own private lives. Ronald Rolheiser puts it this way:

> We can be morally impeccable within our private lives (churchgoing, prayerful, kind, honest, gentle, and generous in our dealings with others) and still, at the same time, unknowingly, participate in and help sustain (through our work, our political affiliations, our economic ideology, our investments, and simply by our consumeristic lifestyle) systems which are far from charitable, gentle, prayerful, and moral.[3]

We are called to charity toward our neighbor in need. And, as the group recognized in offering solutions to the problems, for those who are overlooked or fall under the radar screen more than charity is required. It requires a larger view, a wider horizon that can take in both individual situations and the cultural, economic, educational, social and political systems that foster overlooking a poor man like a Lazarus. This is what the church calls social justice. Again quoting Father Rolheiser: "To practice social justice is to examine, challenge, refuse as far as possible to participate in, and try to change those systems (economic, social, political, cultural, mythic, and religious) that unjustly penalize some even as they unjustly reward others."[4]

For Christians the desire to seek social justice is motivated and energized by Jesus' call to help build his kingdom of peace and joy for all. "Thy Kingdom come," we pray. In Jesus' tradition and ours, the quest for social justice has been there from the beginning. In Genesis, the first book of the Bible, we learn that God made all people equal in dignity, that all human beings are co-responsible with God for the protection and the stewardship of creation. "And it was so. God saw everything that he had made, and indeed, it was very good" (Genesis 1:30–31).

The Psalmist marveled that God gave human beings stewardship over creation:

> When I look at your heavens, the work of your fingers,
> the moon and the stars that you have established;
> what are human beings that you are mindful of them,
> mortals that you care for them?
>
> Yet you have made them a little lower than God,
> and crowned them with glory and honor.
> You have given them dominion over the works of your hands;
> you have put all things under their feet. (Psalm 8:3–6)

The Hebrew prophets reminded their people that the justice was measured by how well they treated the widows, orphans and strangers—those on the outside.

> For if you truly amend your ways and your doings, if you truly act justly one with another, if you do not oppress the alien, the orphan, and the widow, or shed innocent blood in this place, and if you do not go after other gods to your own hurt, then I will dwell with you in this place, in the land that I gave of old to your ancestors forever and ever. (Jeremiah 7:5–7)

In Matthew 25:31–46 Jesus is at his straightforward best. He tells us that how we treat the hungry, thirsty, alien, imprisoned, sick and poor will judge us. "Truly, I tell you, just as you did it to one of the least of these who are members of my family, you did it to me."

The challenge is clear. We need to expand our horizons to include the strangers, widows, orphans, sick, poor, imprisoned—all the people who "no longer count." Not only do we have to include them in the company of people we are concerned about and care for, but also we have to respond to them in charity and with justice. That means we have to dig into the systems that keep them at such disadvantage as we address their immediate needs and concerns.

In recent times, the church and its teachers have spelled out the implications of this challenge for men and women in business. The Second Vatican Council's Pastoral Constitution on the Church in the Modern World, *Gaudium et spes* says:

> The ultimate and basic purpose of economic production does not consist merely in an increase of the goods produced, nor profit nor prestige; it is directed to the service of man, of man that is, in his totality, taking into account his material needs and the requirements of his intellectual, moral, spiritual, and religious life; of all men whomsoever and of every group of men of whatever race or whatever part of the world. Therefore, economic activity is to be carried out in accordance with techniques and methods belonging to the moral order, so that God's design for man may be fulfilled.[5]

Summarizing over 150 years of pastoral teaching, the U.S. bishops spoke out on the issue with their pastoral letter *Economic Justice for All.* That provoked quite a reaction when it was published. Ten years later, they then followed up on that letter with a succinct listing of ten principles drawn from Catholic teaching on economic life called *A Catholic Framework for Economic Life*. As highlighted in many Woodstock conversations, several of those principles (1, 2, 3, 5, 6 and 9) are quite relevant for those who want to do the right thing in their business activities, day in and day out:

- The economy exists for the person, not the person for the economy (1).
- All economic life should be shaped by moral principles. Economic choices and institutions must be judged by how they protect or undermine the life and dignity of the human person, support the family, and serve the common good (2).
- A fundamental moral measure of any economy is how the poor and vulnerable are faring (3).
- All people have a right to economic initiative, to productive work, to just wages and benefits, to decent working conditions as well as to organize and join unions or other associations (5).
- All people, to the extent they are able, have a corresponding duty to work, a responsibility to provide for the needs of their families, and an obligation to contribute to the broader society (6).
- Workers, owners, managers, stockholders, and consumers are moral agents in economic life. By our choices, initiative, creativity, and investment, we enhance or diminish economic opportunity, community life, and social justice (9).[6*]

When the list of ten principles came out, Woodstock Business Conference participants across the country were asked to consider and give their reactions. The most significant response was the recognition that horizons need to expand because by our "choices, initiative, creativity and investments," we "enhance or diminish economic opportunity, community life, and social justice." Members agreed that what they needed to know and care about had to expand, including the disenfranchised and the economically irrelevant of society and the systems that put them there. They said that they wanted to see with Jesus' eyes and act with Jesus' heart.

**A Catholic Framework for Economic Life* is reproduced in its entirety in Appendix 3.

Exercise

How have you and your organizations recognized those in need, those outside the economic system? Set aside a time to consider the question of expanding your horizon to include the disenfranchised and those who don't count in society.

1. Take time to quiet and compose yourself.

2. Pray for the grace to see and hear the truth.

3. Read aloud the parable of the rich man and Lazarus (Luke 16:19–31) and reflect quietly on this familiar story.

4. Consider and discuss the following questions:
   - By any standard we are economically favored. What does this mean for me, for my company, for those I am responsible for, for those I encounter?
   - In my work, can I or can my organization recognize or have concern for the poor, foreigners, widows, orphans, those who have no one to stand up for them?
   - How have I been a steward of what has been given to me, for all of God's creation?

5. Take stock of what you considered as you reflected on the Scripture passage and the questions. Tell our Lord what struck you. Anything new? Anything you want to do? Ask him for the grace to move forward.

6. Give thanks to God for any insights you came to. End by praying Saint Ignatius' Prayer for Generosity.

> *Lord, teach me to be generous.*
> *Teach me to serve you as you deserve;*
> *to give and not to count the cost,*
> *to fight and not to heed the wounds,*
> *to work hard and not to seek rest,*
> *to put myself out and not to ask for reward,*
> *save that of knowing that I do your will.*
> *Amen.*

CHAPTER 9

ENGAGEMENT

Find God in the Opportunities at Hand

The last chapter examined the dynamic moving us to expand our horizons to include all of God's creation, particularly as we encounter those who we might otherwise overlook, those on the economic fringes of society. The focus was on social justice at work. The need for horizon expansion is not limited to purely economic concerns. Seeing with Jesus' eyes takes in much more.

Pope John Paul II emphasized this during his January 10, 2005, meeting with the diplomatic corps accredited to the Holy See. He said that life, food, peace and freedom, particularly religious freedom, are the four most urgent challenges now facing humanity.[1] He implored the governments of the world, and each of us, to expand our horizons, to enlarge what we know and care about, including the worldwide challenge to life, "particularly the beginning of human life" and to the family.[2] He asked us to be mindful of the "hundreds of millions of human beings suffering from grave malnutrition" and the "million of children who every year die of hunger or its effects." He grieved, "How many wars and armed conflicts continue to take place—between states, ethnic groups, peoples and groups living in the same territory. From one end of the world to the other, they are claiming countless innocent victims and spawning so many other evils!"[3]

No Lack of Problems

The breadth of problems confronting our businesses, society and world can be daunting, overwhelming. But, for some reason, we are not frozen by the challenge. Indeed, let us return briefly to the focus of the Woodstock Business Conference meeting introduced in the last chapter. That was a discussion about recognizing those in our society who are ignored because they lack the ability to contribute economically. The engagement by members of the group did not end with recognition of a problem, a moral and ethical problem. They moved quickly to suggest solutions, steps that they, their organizations and the Woodstock group itself might take to ameliorate the situation. They were moved to engagement as one can see listening to some additional excerpts from the meeting we visited in the last chapter:[4]

- The issue is that businesses are not going to employ uneducated people who live in ghettos and who don't appear to be looking for work. There's nothing to draw businesses to these people. So what is the Christian businessperson's role in this situation? Should we go find some people, bring them in, train them and make them economically relevant? I saw a television report recently that presented examples of businesses that are doing this sort of thing. In our country, the corporations are where most economic power resides. They can change things because they have the resources.
- Voluntary action may not increase total employment; I'm not saying we can prevent downsizing. But, I think we need to draw into the system some of those who are simply outside of it now. My company does this by hiring people, giving them scholarships to school and so on.
- The scale of the problem is bigger than voluntary efforts can handle. Administration is done better by private institutions, but the government is the only institution that can raise enough money.
- No one element will solve the problem—government, corporations, individuals. Obviously, we need some kind of combination. You start by working on what's

closest to you, and then you identify bridges between the various levels.

- If there is a corporate program for training people, I think the most important thing is for the executives themselves to get involved in hands-on work in the program. That's when a new understanding of the problem will occur.
- We're not sufficiently humble to recognize how lucky we are. The children of the earlier generations of immigrants did well because they came from solid families. The family gave them a sense of meaning. We want our lives to mean something, whether it's religious life, being in business, raising a family or whatever. The children in this group we're talking about need one-to-one mentoring. Organizations as such aren't enough; only another person can help give one of these kids a sense of meaning. We need something like a national service corps of mentors.

Hearing these men and women, we get an immediate sense that it is not enough to recognize a problem or even identify the problem as a moral or ethical one. While that is a necessary first step, they were compelled to engage the problem, to brainstorm solutions, to involve their companies and themselves in tackling the question in order to make things better. Thus, we see that the next essential pillar of the five-point plan is just that, engagement.

Engagement describes an attitude, a commitment, as well as the day-to-day activities of a calling or profession. The good we can do at work and at home for family, individuals and for society is far too important to ignore. We are all called to collaborate in God's creative and redemptive work, called to use our skills and talents for the greater good. Human activity properly lies within the framework of the collaboration with

God that every human being is called to. Today we are called to echo this divine design and collaborate with our Creator in the transformation of the world according to his plan.

The notion of our collaboration with God conveys the idea that human work is a sharing in the divine work of creation. Pope John Paul II stressed this idea in his writings, time and time again. By our proper use of the wealth of spiritual and material resources given to us by the Creator, we are called to contribute to the progress of society.

The obvious implication of this call to collaborate is that we should not run away and hide. We can neither withdraw from society nor deny our Christian values at work by constructing barriers to seal off concerns generated by our religious sensibilities. That can be self-defeating and unhealthy. We hear that compartmentalization is quite popular today. Seeing one's life as a kind of vocation or calling is one way to gain the attitude, disposition and commitment necessary to answer the call to collaborate with God in his work. The task at hand is to bring one's whole self (mind, heart and soul) to each day's challenges and opportunities wherever they might be found. Each of the above quotes from Woodstock Business Conference members demonstrates that the call to engagement is very much a part of the fire that drives us.

What Kind of Engagement?

In his encyclical *Laborem exercens*, Pope John Paul II taught that despite all the toil that defines human work—and "perhaps, in a way, because of it"—work is good for us as individuals and good for humanity. "Because through work man not only transforms nature, adapting it to his own needs, but he also achieves fulfillment as a human being and indeed in a sense becomes more a human being."[5]

So we engage at our work and with all that we know and

care about. We work within our horizons and we exercise our abilities. In order to do all this and do it well we must:

- Be awake, attentive and aware.
- Be intelligent and informed.
- Value what is good, worthwhile and true.
- Decide capably.
- Act in a planned and rational way.[6]

We must roll up our sleeves in imitation of Our Lord, "who, while being God, became like us in all things devoting most of the years of his life on earth to manual work at the carpenter's bench."[7]

Much of the work over the last twenty years by Woodstock Theological Center scholars features an exploration of the thought of Bernard Lonergan, S.J., and its implications on their various projects. In *Method in Theology* Lonergan described how we come to know and choose what to do. He points the way to a faith-informed approach to engagement, a dynamic process embedded in each human. He describes the process of how we know and operate when we operate at our best.

Lonergan's process begins with our searching for, paying attention to and understanding all the relevant facts. As this stage matures, we come to a judgment as to how best to explain the situation, event or occurrence. Immediately we move forward to understand and judge the values that are at stake. With a grasp of the values involved, we move finally to acts of decision and implementation. This set of actions often proceeds so fluidly and so swiftly that we only notice the end result. However, beneath what might seem to be a smooth arc from initial impulse to action lays a series of connected operations. Good ethical decisions and healthy engagement occur when the acts at each stage along the path are performed well. Conversely, when we fall short we find that one or more of the operations in the series is neglected. Laziness, aimlessness, self-absorption, fear and timidity all can cause us to fall short, to squander our gifts.

Heroism, Ingenuity and Love

Chris Lowney, author of *Heroic Leadership*, found a number of distinctive qualities that promote and reinforce healthy engagement. Four pillars stand in Lowney's scheme of things for effective, world-changing engagement. In addition to *self-awareness* they are *heroism*, *ingenuity* and *love*.

HEROISM

According to Lowney, a certain restless energy marked the early Jesuit enterprise. Its members reached for the stars. They internalized an aggressive drive to imagine whether there was not some even greater project to be accomplished or some better way of attacking the problem at hand. They called it the *magis*, which meant always going for the more, stretching for something greater, going further still than wholehearted service.[8] They internalized Ignatius of Loyola's urging to do what needed to be done without being satisfied with doing it halfway.

Lowney maintains that the built-in energy of the *magis* and the internalized desire of the early Jesuits to pursue some better approach or some worthier challenge made their engagement with the world one that was *magis*-driven and, therefore, led to heroic consequences.

> *Magis*-driven leadership inevitably leads to heroism. Heroism begins with each person considering, internalizing and shaping his or her mission. Whether one works within a large organization or alone, no mission is motivating until it is personal. And it is sustainable only when one makes the search for *magis* a reflexive daily habit. A *magis*-driven leader is not content to go through the

> motions or settle for the status quo but is restlessly inclined to look for something more, something greater. Instead of wishing circumstances were different, *magis*-driven leaders either make them different or make the most of them. Instead of waiting for opportunities, they find gold in the opportunities at hand.[9]

INGENUITY

"Ingenuity disposes people not just to think outside the box but to live outside the box," Lowney concludes.[10] As the habit of pursuing the *magis* and always stretching for the more was the foundation for heroic goals and actions, Lowney maintains that the ingenious strategies and tactics of his Jesuit heroes depended on their having cultivated the "vital attitude of indifference—the lack of inordinate attachments."[11] He explains:

> Indifference leads people to root out provincialism, fear of the unknown, attachment to their own status or possessions, prejudice, aversion to risk, and the attitude that "we've always done it this way." And when people see the whole world as their home, they can turn a hopeful, interested, and optimistic gaze toward new ideas, cultures, places, and opportunities. By freeing themselves from inordinate attachments that could inhibit risk taking or innovation, they became poised to pounce imaginatively on new opportunities.[12]

Ingenuity, a quality needed for successful engagement, for pouncing imaginatively on opportunities, is rarely inborn but is developed over time by cultivating the vital attitude of indifference. That attitude is captured in Saint Ignatius' prayer:

> *Take, Lord, and receive all my liberty,*
> *my memory, my understanding, and my entire will.*
> *All I have and call my own.*
> *You have given all to me,*

to you, Lord, I return it.
Everything is yours; do with it what you will.
Give me only your love and your grace,
That is enough for me.

LOVE

The third essential ingredient for constructive engagement is love. Love drives action. According to Lowney, "Love lends purpose and passion to ingenuity and heroism."[13] How is this?

- Love allows a company to embrace all talent, regardless of creed, color, social status or credentials.
- Love is the passion to see team members excel, "to run at full speed towards perfection."
- And love is the glue that binds individuals into loyal, supportive teams.

Love-driven leaders see a world of uniquely dignified humans, not "fearful, greedy deceivers." They live by the premise that people perform their best when working with and for people who offer genuine support and affection.[14]

Our purposeful engagement at work and in the world when driven by love is but a reflection of the fact that we are loved into being and sustained by God's love. See the difference it makes just by looking at the points drawn from Lowney's analysis. Love allows us to see beyond the roadblocks that would keep us from engaging with and enjoying the talents and gifts of others. It is the basis for true teamwork. It is the motivation for us to empower others so that they can realize the fullness of their potential. God loves perfectly. We cannot, but we can try and in trying, we appreciate ourselves as loved by God; and we desire to make the most of our gifts and avoid squandering them. We desire that our engagement will be aligned with God's plan and reach for God's goals for us and his world.

Exercise

1. Give thanks to God for the time to consider how you act or react when confronting a problem or issue related to your work.

2. Ask for the grace to see your attitudes and habits as they are at your work and elsewhere.

3. Imagine yourself there among Jesus' disciples, fearful and hiding in a safe place after his death and resurrection. You are there in the safe room away from the crowds when the Holy Spirit breaks in. Then the disciples, led by Peter, explode out onto the streets of Jerusalem to engage the crowds and the authorities and to take the message of salvation through Jesus to the world. Read Acts 2:1–13, the account of the coming of the Holy Spirit upon the disciples at Pentecost. Read it slowly and aloud. Pause when something hits you.

4. How would you describe the way the disciples responded and engaged the world? How have you engaged when you are at your best at work?

- Are you awake, attentive and aware?
- Are you intelligent and informed?
- Do you value what is good, worthwhile and true?
- Do you make decisions capably?
- Do you act in a planned and rational way?
- Are you rolling up your sleeves and diving in, in imitation of our Lord?
- Do you see heroism, ingenuity and love at work as you engage the world?

5. Tell God what you learned and what you would like to do to follow up. Ask for the grace to keep at it.

6. In thanksgiving, pray Saint Ignatius' prayer *Take, Lord, and Receive.*

CHAPTER 10

COMMUNITY

The fourth essential element in our five-point program is community. In today's secular culture being a person who affirms that one's religious faith informs one's life can be very lonely. We seek integration and the strengthening of relationships with God, others and the world. We want something more than skillfully silencing or bracketing off our religious concerns at work. What we are seeking requires communities of support and encouragement. Our Catholic faith community—going back in time, embedded in the present and facing the future—can help to channel and encourage our desire to do what is right, to be good disciples. Following are four different kinds of communities that sustain and foster our doing the right thing in business and in the world. The categories into which these examples fall range widely: a businessperson's group, a prayer group, a support group and a worshiping faith community.

Four Communities

WOODSTOCK BUSINESS CONFERENCE

Business and professional men and women gather for many purposes. One group, the Woodstock Business Conference, has as a part of its mission helping participants integrate their faith, family and professional lives. The Conference is described at length in Appendix 1, including its history, process, organization, underlying theory and results. The group's stories and insights are sprinkled throughout this book. They should demonstrate the deep impact that participation in the Woodstock monthly gatherings has had on the participants. The shared narratives in each Woodstock chapter help form a community of men and women and aid them in their quest to do the right thing at work.

PRAYER GROUP

Prayer groups and Bible-study gatherings have been around for many years. A good example of the latter is an effort that began a little over twenty years ago. Our pastor inaugurated a program for a number of small, Scripture-based prayer groups to be located in people's homes throughout the parish. Typically, these groups gather on a weekly basis during Advent and Lent to reflect on the Sunday Gospel. The format is very simple: The group gathers for a brief social time; is then called to prayer with a reading or music or period of silence; the Sunday Gospel is read for the first time; and, participants respond reflecting on what they heard or felt, how the passage struck them in their lives that day. Often, participants will recount the points made or those that the preachers should have been made in homilies heard the Sunday before. After the discussion, the Gospel is read a second time and people pray over it. The meeting generally concludes with the Lord's Prayer.

These Scripture-based prayer groups continue to form in our parish each Advent and Lent. Some have been in continuous operation, meeting biweekly during Ordinary Time, for almost twenty years, with fresh faces joining every season. Participants give testimony to the power of the prayer groups as they witness to the parish community before new sign-up seasons. They recount how participation has been for them life-giving and faith-deepening. New insights result when the richness of the Gospel is shared with such seriousness and groundedness. They say it has inspired them. Community and friendships are formed. Support is there in times of need and sorrow, as is celebration in times of happiness and joy. Shared opportunities for spiritual growth are explored. Friends are there to hold each other to account.

Other than the very simple format, the logistics of finding people to open their homes for the meetings and helping new participants find their groups, there is no official leadership, agenda or cost. The aim of wholeness, integrity and deepened spirituality is realized by openness to the Spirit grounded in prayerful reflection on the Word of God.

MEN'S AND WOMEN'S SUPPORT GROUPS

Estrangement and isolation, products of intense time pressures at work and home, only heighten our need for communities of support. Such communities take many forms. Men's and women's support groups for individuals caught up in the seemingly limitless demands and responsibilities of family and business have grown in popularity over the last twenty years. One particular example is a men's group that formed about seventeen years ago.

At a family weekend retreat sponsored by our parish, one of the men, a psychiatrist, posted a notice that read: "Men's Group Meeting after lunch" and gave the location. At the meeting, he began by asking the assembled group a series of questions:

- How many of you had a best buddy when you were a boy, someone you shared everything with, secrets and all? *All hands went up.*
- What about when you were a teenager? *Most hands went up.*
- How many of your wives have a best friend now, another woman she confides in? *Again, most hands went up.*
- How many of you now have a best buddy or friend, other than your wife, that you can talk things over with, talk about what is happening at work, with the family, with your faith, about things that really matter? *No hands.*

Then he said: "That might give us a clue why women are outliving men."

After exploring the implications of this informal survey in terms of friendships, health and quality of life, the men in the group promised to learn each other's names and meet once a month for the next six months to see what would happen.

They kept their promise and began monthly meetings. Soon, it was clear that once a month was too infrequent; they decided to meet every two weeks. The ground rules they developed were quite simple. Almost every other Saturday someone offers his home for the early morning meeting. It begins at 7:30 and ends at 9:00 A.M. Another signs up to bring the bagels and donuts and a third brings fruit juice. Coffee is the responsibility of the morning's host. Three or four times a year a mailing is sent with the dates, locations and responsibilities for the upcoming months. Now all this is handled by E-mail.

As time went on new men came in at the invitation of a friend and stayed. The E-mail list has over seventy-five entries. Some members move on and reconnect when back in town. Others who find themselves unable to make meetings for some time return and express amazement that they can find themselves right back at home again.

There is no fixed agenda, there are no officers and there are no dues. The meeting generally begins with each person stating his name. The discussion takes off almost spontaneously. What the group has done over time is build friendships and community within a context of shared spiritual values. The discussions involve personal sharing about life's milestones and contemporary challenges, as they are experienced in the day to day. Prayer lives, faith concerns, matters relating to children and parents, work and jobs, and even larger societal issues are often grist for the mill. The quality of listening is profound. Men support each other as they try to live Christian values at work, in family, personal relationships and in the larger community. Meetings have seen expressions of the deepest wisdom and the most poignant stories. Above all, the Saturday morning meetings are marked with hearty, loud, full-bodied laughter.

The men's group meetings have produced some visible offshoots like weekend retreats, Christmas parties, numerous hands-on projects. But the most important product has been friendships—sometimes life-saving friendships—that have formed and deepened over the years. Through the process members of the men's group have come to fuller wholeness and deeper integrity.

WORSHIPING FAITH COMMUNITY

The fourth and most profound example is that of a worshiping faith community. Participating in a worshiping faith community is one of Father Rolheiser's four nonnegotiables for a healthy spiritual life. A major thrust of his book *The Holy Longing* is his persuasive showing of the absolute necessity of community in one's spiritual quest. He says, "Spirituality is not a private search for what is highest in oneself but a communal search for the face of God. The call of God is double: Worship divinity and link yourself to humanity."[1] He points out that Jesus was quite certain on this:

> He teaches us clearly that God calls us, not just as individuals, but as community and that how we relate to each other is just as important religiously as how we relate to God. Or, more accurately, how we relate to each other is part of how we relate to God. For Jesus, the two great commandments, to love God and love one's neighbor, can never be separated.[2]

Those who divorce their search for God from involvement within a church community miss one of the "primary demands inherent right within the very quest of God.... Spirituality is about a communal search for the face of God—and one searches communally only within a historical community."[3] Quoting Jesus in Matthew 18:20, "For where two or three are gathered in my name, I am there among them," Rolheiser says that we have to take Jesus' promise literally:

> Christian life is not sustained only by private acts of prayer, justice, and virtue. It is sustained in a community, by gathering ritually around the word of God and through the breaking of the bread. However, it is important to understand that this kind of gathering is not simply a social one, capable only of doing what social gatherings can do. To gather around the word of God and the breaking of the bread is a ritual gathering and ritual brings something that normal social gatherings do not, namely, transformative power beyond what can be understood and explained through the physical, psychological, and social dynamics that are present.[4]

Christianity has sustained itself for two thousand years through the ritual gathering around the Word of God and the breaking of the bread. The aim of the Mass, the eucharistic liturgy, transcends those of exemplary groups like the support group, prayer group or Woodstock Business Conference. According to Rolheiser, the purpose of the Eucharist is not:

> [T]o have a family or community meeting, or to discuss our emotions and problems, or to seek communal therapy, or even to rally our faltering faith in a pagan world. We gather to communally worship God and let God do in us what we cannot do within ourselves, namely, give us faith and shape us into a community beyond our conflicting emotional pulls and the things we need therapy for.[5]

When we gather around the Word of God and share the breaking of the bread, our Christian community, in worship together, lets God channel the fire within us and enables the Holy Spirit to shape and propel us on the course to do the right thing at work and in the rest of our lives.

There is evil and sin in the world. We all sin, fall short of the mark. There are systems and structures at work and in our society that promote evil as well as those that support goodness and justice. Alone, we might easily overlook the absurdity of evil and sin. Alone, we might lack the power to confront the structures or systems at work that encourage evil. But within a worshiping faith community we are spurred to recognize what we would otherwise overlook and to question what might otherwise remain buried by ignorance or prejudice. The various communities described here are quite different in their particular aims and the composition of the membership. Nevertheless, they highlight the sustaining power of community in our quest for wholeness and integrity.

Being alone whether physically or psychologically can be quite unhealthy. It conflicts with who we are, how we grow and who we are meant to be. We need others.

Taking a step back, we can see that our obvious limitations are also a part of God's plan. The *Catechism of the Catholic Church* underscores the fact that our limitations are not without purpose:

> On coming into the world, man is not equipped with everything he needs for developing his bodily and spiritual life. He needs others. Differences appear tied to age, physical abilities, intellectual or moral aptitudes, the benefits derived from social commerce, and the distribution of wealth [Cf. GS 29 § 2]. The "talents" are not distributed equally [Cf. *Mt* 25:14-30; *Lk* 19:11-27].[6]

> These differences belong to God's plan, [God] who wills that each receive what he needs from others, and that those endowed with particular "talents" share the benefits with those who need them. These differences encourage and often oblige persons to practice generosity, kindness, and sharing of goods; they foster the mutual enrichment of cultures.[7]

Our path toward doing the right thing in our jobs and in the world calls for self-understanding, expanding our horizons, engagement and community. All help us to share our "talents," to practice generosity and grow in wholeness and integrity. Ours are busy days, but the members of these groups choose to join with each other, to form community. In collaboration, we foster the habits and practices that promote healthy integration and wholeness. It is in community that we learn to channel the fire within and to allow the Holy Spirit to guide and support us as we strive to do the right thing. As Father Rolheiser observes, "In an age when it is so difficult to sustain faith and to sustain community, there can be no better advice to us than that of Jesus himself: Gather around the word of God and break bread together."[8]

Exercise

1. After setting aside time for quiet, ask God for the grace to see his presence in your life and in the communities that have helped support and sustain you.

2. Read and consider Saint Catherine of Siena's meditation on the necessity of our individual limitations. She hears God say:

> I distribute the virtues quite diversely; I do not give all of them to each person, but some to one, some to others.... I shall give principally charity to one; justice to another, humility to this one, a living faith to that one.... And so I

> have given everything to such diversity that I have not given everything to one single person, so that you may be constrained to practice charity towards one another.... I have willed that one should need another and that all should be my ministers in distributing the graces and gifts they have received from me.[9]

3. Identify the communities in your life where you have found and extended support and friendship, where you have experienced a sharing of gifts and graces.

- Describe the group and its distinctive qualities.
- Remember the individuals involved. Recall some particular instances or events where gifts were shared with you and where you offered your gifts to others.
- Relive any feelings or movements within you as you retrieve these instances of community.

4. Return in prayer to thank God for your communities. Share with God anything you have been prompted to do or say as a result.

5. Pray, in thanksgiving, Saint Francis' Prayer Before the Crucifix:

> *Most high, glorious God,*
> *enlighten the darkness of my heart*
> *and give me, Lord,*
> *a correct faith, a certain hope,*
> *a perfect charity, sense and knowledge,*
> *so that I may carry out your holy and true command.*
> *Amen.*

CHAPTER 11
PRAYER

For Christians prayer is the prerequisite for each of the prior four points in the five-point program. It is essential for wholeness and integrity, for nurturing us in our quest to do the right thing. Regular prayer, both private and communal, sustains us in finding and following our moral compass. Prayer aligns us with the fire of God's Spirit within us. Prayer is also one of Rolheiser's four nonnegotiable practices for a healthy Christian spirituality. He convincingly asserts that:

> [F]rom what is best in Christian and secular tradition, we hear the truth that sustaining a life of faith, and a balanced life in general, depends upon developing a habit of private prayer. Moreover, as the same sources assure us, we should not expect this to be easy. All the things that work against our faith also work against developing the habit of private prayer. We must, however, continue to try, continue to consistently set a time to spend apart with God.[1]

The spiritual writer and theologian Michael Downey agrees. He submits that from a Christian perspective living a good moral and ethical life requires individual and communal prayer. At the same time, our efforts to live such a life give shape to our prayer.[2]

We are far from alone in our desire to do the right thing at work or any other aspect of our lives. In fact, we are loved by God into being and empowered in life by God's grace. As Catholics, we respond at Eucharist. We give thanks. Through prayer we keep our communication lines with God open and supple.

We often mistakenly think that in our attempts to connect with God the initiative is in our hands. True, we are in search of God. But God always calls us first to conversation and communion. Our prayer, being in communication with God, raising our minds and hearts to God, is always in the first instance a response to the initiative taken by God who lovingly calls to us. The *Catechism* puts it this way:

> *God calls man first.* Man may forget his Creator or hide far from his face; he may run after idols or accuse the deity of having abandoned him; yet the living and true God tirelessly calls each person to that mysterious encounter known as prayer. In prayer, the faithful God's initiative of love always comes first; our own first step is always a response. As God gradually reveals himself and reveals [us to ourselves], prayer appears as a reciprocal call, a covenant drama. Through words and actions this drama engages the heart.[3]

Prayer along with other spiritual practices like meditation, contemplation and asceticism, is, according to Michael Downey, a response to the Spirit, that is, a "means of bringing about ever fuller participation in the life of God and God's providential plan for creation."[4] He explains:

> Christian spirituality develops through the life of prayer, which is the ongoing cultivation of relationship with God rooted in God's being toward us. The spiritual life is sustained and flourishes by the continuing call of the God who is recognized as active in history and present to creation, and by gradual appropriation of the salvific gift offered in the life and ministry, crucifixion and resurrection of Christ.[5]

Can our work be our prayer? Emilie Griffin enjoyed a very successful career as an advertising executive before embarking on her second profession as a prolific author of books and articles on the spiritual life. She maintains that with the right attitude and disposition on our part our prayer and work can become so intertwined that separation becomes difficult if not impossible. She has written a superb book, *Doors Into Prayer: An Invitation*.[6] In it she writes:

> We notice in Scripture that God seems to care about the ordinary things we do. Even our work can lead us closer to God. Do we really believe this? We have had this tendency to divide our work-lives from our home-lives and our prayer-lives. But work, that is, professional work, occupies a huge amount of our time.... We can't afford to look at the majority of our time and call it secular, saying these activities belong to a world outside of God. We need God in all our lives, in our work as in our rest and leisure.
>
> If we take the right attitude and develop the right disposition, our prayer and our work can be intertwined. We can be conscious of God's blessing in everything we do. And our work can become a prayer when we offer it to God.[7]

Which prayer practices can help us to achieve the right attitude and develop the right disposition so that our work can become a prayer offered to God? The array of prayer forms and practices is limitless. Traditional categories include blessings, adoration, petitions, lamentations, intercession, thanksgiving and praise. There is vocal prayer, meditation, contemplation, reading, pondering Sacred Scripture and active participation in the liturgy of the church. The benefits of small faith-sharing groups, spiritual direction and the charisms of our religious orders point the way to fuller, more fruitful prayer opportunities.

I have had the good fortune to work with a wonderful collection of men and women in religious orders: Jesuits,

Franciscans, Carmelites, Augustinians, Redemptorists, Sacred Hearts and Oblates of Saint Francis de Sales to name but a few. The women and men in religious orders are great assets for the church and for each of us. Over the years men and women in religious life have led the church in times of trouble and corruption to renewal and greater spiritual health. We all know about Saints Francis and Clare, Dominic, Catherine of Siena, Benedict, Teresa of Avila, Thérèse of Lisieux, Ignatius of Loyola, Francis de Sales and Jane de Chantal. We can claim a wonderful family of generous people in our church who made and make a difference because of their prayers. They support us in ours.

While no particular form or method of prayer can be said to be specifically tailored for a busy businessperson or professional, the rich tradition with which we are blessed suggests some practices or disciplines that suit those fully engaged in the world of work and family.

Wasting Time with God During the Day

Time is always a problem. We need to build the habit of scheduling a few moments in our work day, at the start or during the day, when we can take a time to be present to God, to open the windows and let God's loving desire for our company into our hearts. It is best to have a regular time and place. We should use that dedicated time to pray in whatever way works. Examples include daily Mass, imaginative prayer, meditative prayer (such as pondering the Scripture readings for the day), centering prayer, praying the Psalms, praying before icons or holy pictures and praying the rosary. We need to reflect and to deepen our sense of gratitude.

Review of the Day

Earlier we discussed the Examen, that prayer practice of reviewing the day beginning in gratitude for benefits and graces received in order to see and relive the occasions of grace and those where improvement is called for. *What did I see? What did I feel? Where did I find God?* This daily review opens our eyes so that we can live and act in the present, where God wants us to work with him for the good of all his creation, so that his kingdom of love, peace and justice will come. (See Appendix 2.)

We also need to probe our own religious faith to know God, God's works and God's will for us. Such study can itself be a very positive form of prayer. The same diligence and energy spent in learning what is necessary for our jobs, our markets, our products and services can—when focused on the history, practices and grounding of our religious faith—produce rare and enriching fruit.

Emilie Griffin recalls that she looked for examples of others as she worked to shape her own prayer life. She became so fond of the writings of C.S. Lewis that he became one of her prayer-mentors. Although, "He was certainly scheduled to the hilt...," Lewis managed to find time for prayer in the middle of all his university writing and teaching:

> How did he plan his time to include both prayer and worship? His schedule is well documented. On weekdays he attended services in his college chapel. He sometimes went to weekday services at a nearby church. On Sundays he went to a church near his home. On Thursday evenings in his college rooms he met with a circle of friends who were as keen on God as he was. Over and above this he pursued certain friendships of the heart. J.R.R. Tolkein... Charles Williams....Jesus, one could say, was an unseen third in their twosomes. And Lewis engaged in private prayer. He prayed in odd places, not always quiet places. He was fond of praying on railway journeys. He liked long walks. When he was alone these were good chances for prayer.[8]

Here, Griffin underscores the value of friendships in our pursuit of wholeness and integration as well as the need for ingenuity and discipline in carving out time for prayer.

Our ultimate "prayer-mentor" is Jesus Christ. The Gospels repeatedly show Jesus at prayer before important events in his life like his baptism, the Transfiguration and most memorably in the garden before his passion and death. He prayed before decisive moments in the mission of the disciples. He prayed as he commissioned his apostles and washed their feet the night before his death. He often prayed alone. His disciples saw him at prayer and asked him to teach them how to pray. Our own instruction and inspiration in prayer comes from his life and teaching. In Matthew's Gospel he answers any questions we might have:

> Pray then in this way:
>
> Our Father in heaven,
> hallowed be your name.
> Your kingdom come.
> Your will be done, on earth as it is in heaven.
> Give us this day our daily bread.
> And forgive us our debts, as we also have forgiven our debtors.
> And do not bring us to the time of trial,
> but rescue us from the evil one. (6:9–13)

We say this prayer all the time. We pray for the coming of the kingdom of God. "For the kingdom of God is not food and drink but righteousness and peace and joy in the Holy Spirit" (Romans 14:17). We are on course when we pattern our prayer and our quest for wholeness and integrity after Jesus' example. He brought the kingdom of righteousness, peace and joy in the Holy Spirit. When we follow this perfect model, we are on course, doing the right thing.

Exercise

1. Give thanks to God for his faithful beckoning, his calling you to him.

2. Ask for the grace to open the windows and doors of your consciousness to let in God's desire to be with you and have you with him.

3. Consider your prayer over the past few months. How would you characterize how well you have connected in the midst of all that you have to do each day? Have you wasted time with God? Have you taken a few moments at the end of the day for a review, an *Examen*?

4. Read over Thomas Merton's famous prayer from *Thoughts in Solitude*:

> *My Lord God, I have no idea where I am going.*
> *I do not see the road ahead of me.*
> *I cannot know for certain where it will end.*
> *Nor do I really know myself,*
> *and the fact that I think that I am following your will does not mean that I am actually doing so.*
> *But I believe that the desire to please you*
> *does in fact please you.*
> *And I hope I have that desire in all that I am doing.*
> *I hope that I will never do anything apart from that desire.*
> *And I know that if I do this you will lead me by the right road*
> *though I may know nothing about it.*
> *Therefore will I trust you always*
> *though I may seem to be lost and the in the shadow of death.*
> *I will not fear, for you are ever with me,*
> *and you will never leave me to face my perils alone.*[9]

5. Now tell the Lord what it is that you desire. Ask for the grace to carry out your resolve.

6. Close with the prayer Jesus taught us, the Our Father.

Conclusion
Do Justice, Love Kindness and Walk Humbly with Your God

Recent events, scandals, wars and natural disasters have heightened our desire to focus on what really counts, to return to what is essential and basic in our lives. Our world right now seems to be in the middle of a profound sea change affecting all aspects of life: social, cultural, economic and political. The changes are being played out all over the world. More than ever, people want to integrate their whole selves, who they are with what they do. Those studying what is going on with people at work in America have claimed, with some hyperbole, that Americans have discovered—*the spirituality and work movement.* Observers like Laura Nash at Harvard Business School talk about an "explosion of spirituality in the workplace."

Whether or not there are any explosions or any movements afoot, it is true that we are coming to recognize the deep-seated drive within each one of us to use our talents, intelligence and imagination for the greater good. No one promised us it would be easy. Indeed, many harbor deep-seated doubt that it is even possible in this time of rapid change, shifting boundaries and faint allegiances to lead a spiritual life in the business world. Our age has seen the decline in the loyalty of the organization toward the individual and of workers toward their organizations. It seems now everyone is a free agent. Then, there are the very recent notorious breaches of trust. Trust and trustworthiness seem to be things of the past. We see diminished professionalism in the practice of law and medicine. We see sin and mismanagement in our church. Individualism and selfishness seem to be elevated and rewarded, defeating teamwork and community.

Back in the middle of the first century, Saint Paul wrote his lengthy letter to the people of the church in Rome. His instructions to the Romans included cogent insights and a good deal of ethical wisdom. At one point he told them: "Do not be conformed to this world, but be transformed by the renewing of your minds, so that you may discern what is the will of God—what is good and acceptable and perfect" (Romans 12:2).

Two thousand years later Paul's teaching still rings true. As we work at our jobs, in our families and in our communities, we know that we need to judge what is God's will for us and what is good and acceptable to him, as we discern the right thing to do. Each day when we act in conformity with that judgment, we are carrying God's will for us, cooperating with God in the building of his kingdom.

How can we keep on course to know and do the right thing in the middle of all today's mess? Our faith tells us that this can be done—by finding God who is there at work with us. We can find God when we understand what we are really about at our work.

This is where we come to realize who we are. This is where we spend so much of our day, where we learn by doing to know, choose and do what is best. This is the place where we can truly team up with God. God is already there, working in us and moving us to work for the greater good. We are burning with desire for completeness, for wholeness. We are driven to integrate all of who we are including who and what we are at work. We want to find God as we live our ordinary lives, and doing our ordinary work.

Long ago the prophet Micah berated the leaders of Israel for ripping off people. The leaders were charging people huge sums to have lavish sacrifices. At the same time the leaders led corrupt lives. Greed was their hallmark. Micah predicted horrible consequences. He reminded his listeners that even the most extravagant of offerings to God would not alter the judgments of condemnation the leaders had merited. Then, he offered his famous advice:

> He has told you, O mortal, what is good;
> and what does the LORD require of you
> but to do justice, and to love kindness,
> and to walk humbly with your God? (Micah 6:8)

Whatever our jobs or state of life might be, we carry the challenge to bring justice, kindness and joy to the world. One who is aware of the fire that burns inside is called to a way of being. Our quest for the moral compass, our deep-felt need for integration and wholeness calls us to engage and to live the same values and behaviors in the office, the clinic, the classroom, the courthouse and at home as at church. The five-point program of self-awareness, expanding one's horizons, engagement, community and prayer foster this awareness and burnish this desire.

Our religious faith challenges our notions and behaviors by promoting prayerful reflection and disciplined lives. A religious horizon empowers us to recognize important questions. Our actions affect the lives of those we, and our business organizations, encounter. We learn to notice and evaluate the structures and systems at work. We must engage using our intelligence, our ability to reason, our ability to make and carry out responsible choices and our ability to love. Alone, it is hard to do this well. Community sustains us in a time of change. We are supported by our healthy relationships with our families, friends, neighbors, coworkers and faith communities. We are empowered to stay on the right course when we pray regularly and when we "do justice, love kindness, and walk humbly with [our] God."

NOTES

Introduction

1. February 1994, Woodstock Business Conference, Washington, D.C., Chapter meeting.

Chapter 1

1. The quoted statements in this entire chapter are taken from the November 1998, Woodstock Business Conference, Washington, D.C., Chapter meeting.

Chapter 2

1. Ronald Rolheiser, *The Holy Longing: The Search for a Christian Spirituality* (New York: Doubleday, 1999).
2. Rolheiser, p. 7.
3. Dean H. Hamer, *The God Gene: How Faith Is Hardwired into Our Genes* (New York: Doubleday, 2004).
4. *The Washington Post*, November 13, 2004, p. B9.
5. Michael Downey, *Understanding Christian Spirituality* (Mahwah, N.J.: Paulist, 1997), p. 49.
6. Rolheiser, p. 11.
7. Woodstock Theological Center, *The Ethics of Lobbying: Organized Interests, Political Power, and the Common Good* (Washington, D.C.: Georgetown University, 2002), p. 17.
8. June 1998, Woodstock Business Conference Board meeting.

Chapter 3

1. *Catechism of the Catholic Church, Second Edition* (New York: Doubleday, 1997), #2428.
2. *Catechism of the Catholic Church*, #2427.
3. Austin Flannery, O.P., ed., *Vatican Council II: The Conciliar and Post Conciliar Documents, New Revised Edition*, "Dogmatic Constitution on the Church," *Lumen gentium,* Chapter IV, The Laity (Northport, N.Y.: Costello, 1992), 31.
4. February 1994, Woodstock Business Conference, Washington, D.C., Chapter meeting.

5. February 1994, Woodstock Business Conference, Washington, D.C., Chapter meeting.
6. Woodstock Theological Center, First Annual John T. Garraty Conference on Business Ethics, Prague, Czech Republic, 1997.

Chapter 4

1. James C. Collins and Jerry I. Porras, *Built to Last: Successful Habits of Visionary Companies* (New York: HarperBusiness, 1994).
2. May 1997, Woodstock Business Conference, Washington, D.C., Chapter meeting.
3. Downey, pp. 22–23, 32.
4. Rik Kirkland, Editor's Desk, *Fortune*, July 9, 2001, p. 18.
5. Kirkland, p. 18.
6. Downey, pp. 21–22.
7. Downey, p. 22.
8. See Downey, pp. 23–24.
9. Downey, p. 146.

Chapter 5

1. Pope John Paul II, *Dialogue Between Cultures for a Civilization of Love and Peace: Message for World Day of Peace,* Catholic Information Network, www.cin.org/home/world-day-peace-2001.html., January 1, 2001, pp. 8, 9.
2. This excerpt and the quotations from the first meeting are taken from the October 1997, Woodstock Business Conference, Washington, D.C., Chapter meeting.
3. *Harvard Business Review,* September-October 1998.
4. This excerpt and the balance of the quotations from the second meeting are taken from the October 1998, Meeting of the Woodstock Business Conference Board.
5. "John Paul II's Message to Christian Business Executives," Zenit News Agency, http://zenit.org. March 5, 2004.

6. Bernard J.F. Lonergan, *Method in Theology* (Toronto: University of Toronto, 1990) p. 301.
7. Michael Paul Gallagher, *Clashing Symbols* (Mahwah, N.J.: Paulist, 1998), pp. 12–13.

Chapter 6
1. Zenit, March 6, 2004.
2. *Lumen gentium*, Chapter IV, The Laity, 31.
3. *Lumen gentium*, 36.
4. January 1994, Woodstock Business Conference, Washington, D.C., Chapter meeting.
5. January 1994, Woodstock Business Conference, Washington, D.C., Chapter meeting.
6. October 1993, Woodstock Business Conference, Washington, D.C., Chapter meeting.
7. This excerpt and the meeting quotes that follow are from the January 1994, Woodstock Business Conference, Washington, D.C., Chapter meeting.

Chapter 7
1. This excerpt and the quotes that follow are taken from the June 1998, Woodstock Business Conference, Washington, D.C., Chapter meeting.
2. Chris Lowney, *Heroic Leadership* (Chicago: Loyola, 2003).
3. Rolheiser, p. 53.
4. See Lowney, p. 9.
5. Lowney, p. 27.

Chapter 8
1. This excerpt and the quotes that follow were taken from the February 1996, Woodstock Business Conference, Washington, D.C., Chapter meeting.
2. J. Michael Stebbins, Presentation to Woodstock Business Conference Board, October 14, 1998, Washington, D.C., Chapter meeting.

3. Rolheiser, p. 172.
4. Rolheiser, p. 173.
5. Flannery, "Pastoral Constitution on the Church in the Modern World," *Gaudium et spes,* Chapter III, Economic and Social Life, 64.
6. United States Conference of Catholic Bishops, *A Catholic Framework for Economic Life* (Washington, D.C.: USCCB, 1996).

Chapter 9

1. "John Paul II Highlights Humanity's Four Challenges" in Address to Diplomatic Corps Accredited to the Holy See. Zenit News Service, http://zenit.org, January 10, 2005, p. 1.
2. Zenit, p. 1.
3. Zenit, p. 3.
4. February 1996, Woodstock Business Conference, Washington, D.C., Chapter meeting.
5. John Paul II, *On Human Work, Encyclical Laborem Exercens* (Washington, D.C.: United States Catholic Conference, 1981) pp. 20–21.
6. *Laborem exercens*, 6, p. 13.
7. *Laborem exercens*, 6, p. 14.
8. Lowney, p. 121.
9. Lowney, pp. 243–244.
10. Lowney, p. 281.
11. Lowney, p. 281.
12. Lowney, pp. 281–282.
13 Lowney, p. 282.
14. Lowney, p. 282.

Chapter 10

1 Rolheiser, p. 137.
2 Rolheiser, p. 68.
3 Rolheiser, p. 69.

4. Rolheiser, p. 231.
5. Rolheiser, pp. 236–237.
6. *Catechism,* #1936.
7. *Catechism,* #1937.
8. Rolheiser, p. 237.
9. Saint Catherine of Siena, *Dial.* I, 7, quoted in the *Catechism,* #1937.

Chapter 11

1. Rolheiser, pp. 218–219.
2. Downey, p. 117.
3. *Catechism*, #2567.
4. Downey, p. 46.
5. Downey, p. 147.
6. Emilie Griffin, *Doors Into Prayer: An Invitation* (Brewster, Mass.: Paraclete, 2001), p. 43.
7. Griffin, pp. 43–44.
8. Griffin, pp. 16–17.
9. Thomas Merton, *Thoughts in Solitude* (New York: Farrar, Straus and Giroux, 1958).

APPENDIX 1

WOODSTOCK BUSINESS CONFERENCE

Even recognizing that it is in our work lives, our businesses and our professions that we are called to Christian maturity, hearing that we are called to "contribute to the sanctification of the world" is a tall order. How can we possibly do this in this day and age? An answer, in the form of a process of Christian discernment and decision making, emerged over time with the work of the Woodstock Business Conference. This came about after years of trial and error, meetings, conferences and participation in pilot programs. To set the stage we revisit another meeting. This time it is a fictional recreation fusing many conversations held in different cities over months and years.

It was weekday lunch, as usual, in a bright dining room of the downtown club. Serious-looking, soberly dressed men and women filled the tables. The quiet buzz of conversations about people, events, connections, politics, proposals, markets and deals hummed. One table of five included three highly successful Catholic business leaders, a local pastor and a business professor at the local Catholic university. Each was well known in the local business community. Indeed, as they arrived they were recognized and greeted the occupants of the nearby tables.

The meeting's organizer called together this group of his friends and colleagues. They had a long history together, sharing leadership roles in charitable, civic, university and church matters. Their very comfort with each other laid the foundation for the discussion the organizer proposed. Each took his or her faith seriously, seeing it as penetrating and informing all aspects of life.

The organizer could best be described as a no-nonsense, hard-nosed practical businessman. Not an academic by any stretch of the imagination, he was impatient with philosophizing and what he considered wasteful talk. He had skillfully guided his multinational enterprise though economic ups and downs, the ever-changing buying habits of his customers and the reality of global production of the goods his company sold.

The others included the CEO of a regional financial institution, a solid citizen whose youthful appearance belied his well-earned position as the leader of several local community and church organizations. The third business leader headed a manufacturing concern begun by his father fifty years earlier in New England and that now had facilities across the South and internationally. He was known for his commitment to the university and for his vocal support of liberal policies in the church and society. The university professor taught business ethics and organizational theory. Her provocative articles and engaging lectures made her a favorite on campus, a sought-after business consultant and a well-recognized commentator on radio and TV.

The priest was not only the organizer's pastor and friend; he also had a background in finance and institutional investment before studying for the priesthood. For each, a passionate concern for faith and family shared center stage with the enterprises they ran.

The purpose of the gathering boiled down to consideration of two questions posed by the organizer:

1. "What difference does it make, and for whom, if business leadership is seen as a call for excellence, a call to do God's will?"
2. "How does a business run by a committed Christian differ from any other?"

Participants were reacting to the deluge of high-profile corporate scandals, criminal trials of high-ranking executives and what they saw as a devaluing of ethical business behavior across the board. What were the rules these days? Where could one use one's moral compass and how could that be shared across an organization? One participant cynically put it this way, "It seems that you push the envelope and whatever you do is OK, so long as it is legal or you don't get caught." Another added, "The iron rule of business these days is make your numbers, don't rock the boat and keep your nose clean." All agreed that this "iron rule" contrasted sharply with Christ's law of love: "You shall love the Lord your God with your whole heart, and with all your soul, and with all your mind, and with all your strength.... You shall love your neighbor as yourself" (Mark 12:29–31).

Participants also agreed that business demands constant vigilance by busy people. Time is always an issue. Business people and professionals must ceaselessly attend to their responsibilities, keep their firms viable and growing, meet competition, and, above all, make a profit. How to accomplish this is, of course, where many issues arise. They observed that, "At work, we must account for business decisions to superiors, boards, shareholders, lenders, fellow employees, customers, suppliers and other stakeholders, as well as to outside financial analysts in the case of publicly held companies."

Moreover, they recognized that business enterprise itself plays a fundamental role in public life. This is particularly true today in an age of interdependent commercial and financial global activity. In addressing the needs of their companies, businessmen and businesswomen, entrepreneurs and professionals are constantly making moral decisions that affect not only their own firms and themselves, but also the broader community and society at large. They have to reconcile claims to financial and social prosperity.

Moral issues are ever present. Whether or not anybody explicitly says it, today business people face moral issues coming from all sides. They agreed that they had to draw upon their own convictions, beliefs and experience in deciding what is the right thing to do and affirmed that their ethical and moral values do provide them with guides for decision making.

The initial conversations led to several national conferences, organized by the Woodstock Theological Center that addressed the question of business as a vocation, a call from God. Business leaders, experts in business ethics, church leaders and government officials all participated in the conferences.

A core group of conference participants embarked on a mission to help men and women of faith find the necessary language and encouragement to create organizational cultures and practices consistent with Judeo-Christian values. They initiated a national movement of business leaders and professionals that would meet in local chapters to offer each other a kind of peer ministry in support of that mission. This initiative became known as the Woodstock Business Conference. Its mission statement says:

> The Mission of the Woodstock Business Conference is to establish and lead a national network of business leaders to explore their respective religious traditions in order:
>
> - to integrate faith, family and professional life;
> - to develop a corporate culture that is reflective of their religious values; and,
> - to exercise a beneficial influence upon society at large.
>
> The Conference, grounded in the Roman Catholic tradition, welcomes believers who are open to and respectful of one another's religious traditions. It is committed to the

> conviction that ethics and values grow out of one's religious heritage.

The number of chapters grew over time as men and women continued to meet on a monthly basis and use a tested process that promoted trust, openness, reflection and an ever-deepening understanding of one's calling in the workplace. Participants grew in their ability to have positive impact on their work environment and greater awareness of their roles in the larger society. The Woodstock process exposed practical day-to-day issues confronting busy people within a framework of Scripture readings and topical background articles. The process proved itself in promoting cumulative and progressive understanding, decision making and action grounded in values.

Business and professional people gathered in Woodstock Business Conference chapters to reflect on their religious faith and its meaning and impact of every aspect of their lives. Such gatherings provided important evidence of the convergence of the spiritual quest and the world of work. The process they follow today helps participants realize and appreciate that their ethics and values do in fact grow out of their religious faith. They are able to affirm the relevance of religious faith to business practice, no small feat in our society today.

The introductory material for the Woodstock Business Conference states:

> Conference participants take care to identify values consistent with their religious commitments, to the end that their decisions and actions will be based upon ethical principles informed by and growing out of their religious faith. Religion in general, and particularly the Judeo-Christian tradition, contributes in a number of significant ways:

- thousands of years of prayerful reflection have produced a rich treasure of thought directed to practical resolution of questions of right and wrong;
- the motivational power of religious conviction sustains morally correct behavior;
- a picture of the world emerges from which it makes sense for people to take the dilemmas of moral action seriously and make the effort to do the right thing;
- a way of life is presented which is more comprehensive and demanding; and, a community of believers opens access to a much deeper range of values than those expressed by the conventional wisdom of the day.
- a community of believers also provides needed support for people to do the hard work necessary to get the whole picture to come to good judgments, and to do the right thing.[1]

The Woodstock Process

It would be in order to explain the Woodstock process as it developed and was applied in Woodstock Business Conference meetings. The popularity of the Woodstock Business Conference and programs like it is due, in large measure, to their effectiveness as an answer to our yearning for integration in our lives. They help participants respond positively to our desire to make a difference in our firms and the wider society. People are not satisfied with the status quo. Business executives, managers and professionals want to bridge the apparent gap between faith and work. The Woodstock process combines practical wisdom with theological reflection on the issues and problems of the contemporary workplace.

What is this process and how does it work? Local Woodstock chapter members gather each month to address issues based upon their experience in the workplace. The approach is deceptively simple, but each step is vital to supporting an atmosphere of trust and faith-inspired reflection. The meetings themselves are scheduled to mirror the time, place and surroundings of typical business meetings in a particular community. They generally happen at the same place, date and time each month. The meetings, lasting about one hour and a half, begin on time and end on time so that busy business people can count on and set aside the same time each month.

A format evolved from the experience of business and professional people who began to engage in systematic theological reflection on their lives in the workplace. Over time, its elements and the order of proceeding emerged and were refined. The topics for discussion also developed from the experiences of these chapter meetings.

Taken from the materials published by Woodstock, here are the essential features of each critical element in the process:

1. Introductions. Each meeting begins with everyone present introducing himself or herself. The goal is to build a sense of community and make sure new people are welcome.

2. Opening prayer. Each session begins with a prayer, an acknowledgment that God holds all in existence and gives us the strength to do the right thing. We must have God's grace, light and support to hear his word and learn what to do.

3. Mission statement. Reading the mission statement at the beginning helps keep discussions on track and avoids wasting valuable time. This element was incorporated in response to frustrations experienced in earlier theological reflection groups where participants frequently sought to revisit the purposes for the meeting.

4. Scripture passage and reflection. One of the strengths of the Woodstock process is the period marked by reading a pertinent Scripture passage aloud followed by a five-minute interval of silent reflection. After the silence, participants share how the particular story or image struck them and how the passage applies in life today. The discipline of silence, so rare for many in business, opens new vistas. Woodstock participants report that their appreciation of this phase of the process has grown over time. By entering into our discussions through the threshold of Scripture, we are introduced to the "mind and heart of Christ" and with his sense of purpose and values. His word is the touchstone for the accuracy of what we will decide, as contrasted with popular or conventional wisdom. By proceeding in this manner we expand our horizons. A whole new light shines on the subsequent discussion of marketplace issues.

One participant articulated the richness of this phase:

> I found the few moments of reflection in response to the Scripture to be very, very moving. It would probably be much more difficult to get some insight into the Scripture without this structure or discipline. Reading Scripture this way allows barriers to come down. Scripture allows a common ground for our discussion.

Another added.

> Reading Scripture and reflecting on it helps us to look at our business lives in an entirely different context. The Woodstock meeting is the first time in years or perhaps ever in our lives to just sit down and read the Scripture. What we think about when we take on business issues is different because of the Scripture, whether or not we talk about it during our discussion. And, it often leads right into to the topic we are to discuss at the meeting.

5. Topic. Next comes the topic for the day, i.e., a case, issue, problem or opportunity. An article from the newspaper or a business publication might be offered to help people focus on the concrete details of a particular situation or event. To this focus they bring similar situations from their own experience. The wealth of personal experiences, freely shared within the group, powers the process. Here they also recall the feelings, drives, motivations and concerns associated with the event. While not explicit in the format itself, a series of orderly steps inevitably emerges from the back and forth of the discussion:

- What are the data? What do I see? Necessary data include not only the events themselves, but also all the surrounding circumstances, the people, relationships and communities involved as well as the underlying desires and motivations of the participants.
- What does it mean? We push to understand and explain what is going on. The discussion develops a range of explanations. Hearing different perspectives helps people to come to a fuller understanding of the situation.
- Eventually responsible businesspeople are by training and inclination prompted to "make the call," to name the fact of the matter after due consideration of the explanations offered. And then, we judge "Is this good? "Is it worthwhile?" "Do I like this?"
- What shall I do about it? The final step is deliberation, discernment and decision. Responsibility calls us to respond with some kind of action.

These four steps follow the same pattern in any human activity when we are functioning well, when we are the best we can be. When we can see the pattern at work in ourselves and in the meeting process, it helps us to confirm that we are on the right track. We acknowledge that we are moved through these steps by God's love at work in us. It is the grace we seek, the answer to our prayer.

6. Reflection on the meeting. This important and often unrecognized step in the process takes place in the final five minutes before the end of the meeting. Here, participants are called to stop and reflect on the meeting to see how well or poorly it went. They recall important insights that surfaced and identify issues that warrant further exploration. It is here that chapter members often select the next topic and accept responsibility for its preparation and presentation.

7. Closing prayer. The meeting concludes with prayer, an expression of gratitude. Often it is the Lord's Prayer.

For anyone interested in learning more about the Woodstock Business Conference, joining an existing chapter or helping form a new one, visit its Web page at www.georgetown.edu/centers/woodstock/wbc.htm or contact:

Director
Woodstock Business Conference
Woodstock Theological Center
Georgetown University
P.O. Box 571137
Washington, D.C. 20057-1137
Phone: 202-687-6565
Fax: 202-687-5865

Note

[1] *Introduction to the Woodstock Business Conference*, Washington, D.C., Woodstock Theological Center, p. 3 (March 2003, Edition).

APPENDIX 2

DAILY *EXAMEN* FOR BUSY BUSINESSPEOPLE

Adapted by Martin J. O'Malley, S.J., from the *Spiritual Exercises of Saint Ignatius of Loyola*[1]

1. Thanksgiving
Begin by relaxing into God's presence in an attitude of thankfulness. Find one thing to be thankful for—even if you are having a tough time. Allow gratitude to take hold of you.

2. Pray for Insight
Pray to the Holy Spirit to reveal to you what you need at this time. Consciously open yourself to God's light.

3. Finding God in All Things
This is the heart of the prayer where you examine very concretely the events of the day.

- What happened since the morning?
- Who have you come in contact with?
- What occupies your thoughts today?
- How are you being drawn to God in your life today? Now?
- Where is God calling you specifically this day?
- Is it time to make a tough decision that will affect the lives of many people?
- Should I simply bask in gratefulness to God for my life, career and family?

This is not a time of searching for faults. Rather, it is a chance to take a step back and recognize that God is active in the entirety of the day.

4. Petition
Express to God your desires. Again be specific and frame your prayer here in a petition: "Dear Lord, at this time I ask...for strength to...for courage to...for the resolve to...to be thankful for..."

5. Resolve for the Future
Finally, look to the future. "How shall I live the rest of day?" "What shall I do?"

Finish with a prayer, for example, the Our Father.

Note
[1] Martin J. O'Malley, S.J. *The Corporate Christian: The Soul of a Leader.* (Washington, D.C., Woodstock Theological Center, 2004), p. 62.

APPENDIX 3

A CATHOLIC FRAMEWORK FOR ECONOMIC LIFE[1]

1. The economy exists for the person, not the person for the economy.

2. All economic life should be shaped by moral principles. Economic choices and institutions must be judged by how they protect or undermine the life and dignity of the human person, support the family, and serve the common good.

3. A fundamental moral measure of any economy is how the poor and vulnerable are faring.

4. All people have a right to life and to secure the basic necessities of life (e.g., food, clothing, shelter, education, health care, safe environment, economic security).

5. All people have a right to economic initiative, to productive work, to just wages and benefits, to decent working conditions as well as to organize and join unions or other associations.

6. All people, to the extent they are able, have a corresponding duty to work, a responsibility to provide for the needs of their families, and an obligation to contribute to the broader society.

7. In economic life, free markets have both clear advantages and limits; government has essential responsibilities and limitations; voluntary groups have irreplaceable roles, but cannot substitute for the proper working of the market and the just policies of the state.

8. Society has a moral obligation, including governmental action where necessary, to assure opportunity, meet basic human needs, and pursue justice in economic life.

9. Workers, owners, managers, stockholders, and consumers are moral agents in economic life. By our choices, initiative, creativity, and investment, we enhance or diminish economic opportunity, community life, and social justice.

10. The global economy has moral dimensions and human consequences. Decisions on investment, trade, aid, and development should protect human life and promote human rights, especially for those most in need wherever they might live on this globe.

Note

[1] United States Conference of Catholic Bishops, *A Catholic Framework for Economic Life* (Washington, D.C.: USCCB, 1996).

INDEX

Scripture Index